D1636684

Naturally
Supernatural!

Naturally
Supernatural!

by

Mark & Patti Virkler

© Copyright 1990 by Mark Virkler
ISBN 1-56043-060-5

All rights reserved. This book is protected under the copyright laws of the United States of America. This book may not be copied or reprinted for commercial gain or profit. The use of short quotations or occasional page copying for personal or group study is permitted and encouraged. Permission will be granted upon request. Unless otherwise identified, Scripture quotations are from the New King James Bible, © 1984, by the Thomas Nelson Publishers. Used by Permission. All emphasis within Scripture quotations is the author's addition.

Destiny Image Publishers
P.O. Box 310
Shippensburg, PA 17257

"Speaking to the Purposes of God for this Generation"

For Worldwide Distribution
Printed in the U.S.A.

Inside the U.S. call toll free to order:
1-800-722-6774

This manual is the result of the united efforts of both authors. The concepts and ideas are a culmination of cooperative study and revelation. The experiences described are common to both. The pronoun "I" is used to demonstrate the unity of our thoughts. This is an expansion of, enlargement and addition to the truths found in *Abiding in Christ* by the same authors.

Table of Contents

Introduction

Naturally Supernatural!

Greetings, friends. Today we are going on a journey. Where it will lead is hard to tell, because I am simply going to sit down and tell you a bit of my life's story. I don't really have a clear outline. I suppose that is because my life has not been structured as a clear outline. It was simply lived. I wonder if it is acceptable to tell a story, or if we must force life into clear outlines. I am not sure. Why don't we try it and find out?

I am not going to tell my whole life's story in this book. Instead I want to tell you about one of the central lessons I have learned as I have lived 23 years as a Christian, that of living the "replaced life," or allowing Christ to live His life through me, rather than living myself. I lived as a Christian for twelve years before I discovered this truth. During that time, it was "I" living. Don't be confused and think I was a non-Christian simply doing religious works. No, I had given my life to Jesus at age 15. I had asked Him to be my Lord and Savior, and cleanse me with His shed blood. I was trying as hard as I could to live the Christian life and be pleasing to Him.

For instance, the Bible told me to love my enemies, so I tried as hard as I could (with Christ's help) to do so. I never could quite seem to do it well enough, try and pray as hard as I knew how. It made no difference which biblical command I was trying to obey, I faced the same struggle and the same partial successes and partial failures. It didn't seem that Christianity was **all that supernatural.** I tried as hard as I could and asked God to help me and together we got as far as we got, and that was about it. I couldn't say that I loved my enemies, but I certainly tried.

Then revelation began to pour into my heart. I discovered that "I" no longer lived. I had been crucified and Christ lived! It seemed so hard to accept because when I looked in the mirror, the image I saw certainly looked like me! It took most of a year for the revelation to saturate my heart that I was only a vessel that held Another; that I was a container of the life of Christ; that I was a branch grafted into a Vine. You see, I had grown up thinking that "I" lived, but that was an illusion. Actually, satan, the spirit of this world, had dominion over me. However, since I was not insightful enough to see that, I had grown up believing the illusion that "I" was in control. Now that I was a Christian, I still thought that "I" lived but now Christ was coming alongside me, assisting me in the life I was living.

But again, this was an illusion, because Christ was not only coming alongside to assist me, He was actually going to **be my Life.** "I" was not going to live anymore. I was going to be lost in Him. So many mumble jumble words! It sounded like nice religious jargon. However, it had very little meaning to my life. I looked in the mirror. I saw who was there. It was I, Mark W. Virkler. It was not Jesus. Therefore, all these nice religious platitudes were simply that: religious platitudes. They were not revelation knowledge burning within my heart, transforming my life. They were not experiences. They were trite sayings that did not appear particularly relevant to my walk as a twentieth century Christian.

Then God burned them home. He shone His light upon these confusing, almost meaningless words, and transformed my way of living within. I became supernaturally empowered to live far beyond my own abilities by living out of the life flow within me. I no longer had any limits but began experiencing the limitless power and ability of Almighty God pouring forth through my heart. I became **naturally supernatural!** Christianity took on awesome new prospects. It became much more real than it had ever been before. When I reread the New Testament, it was a new Book. I was seeing it with open eyes for the first time, and I could not believe what I was reading.

This book tells the story of how this revelation broke into my life. It is the story of one who thought he lived, and how God showed him that he had been crucified with Christ, and now Christ lived. It is a story that goes beyond religious platitudes and words, and finds reality in the Person of Christ Jesus our Lord. It is the story of living the replaced life. It is the story of how to begin living naturally in the supernatural. It is testimony to the fact that we as the Church of Jesus Christ are **fused to Glory.**

May you, too, be transformed as you read.

How to Use This Book

This book includes thought and discussion questions at the end of each chapter. I recommend that whenever possible, you study this book with a group that meets together weekly to cover a chapter or two. These groups could be Sunday School classes, home cell groups, women's or men's groups, Bible school classes, Sunday or Wednesday evening services. It could even be a series a pastor preaches through on Sunday mornings. Assign the chapters to be read during the week and come together prepared to discuss the application of the truths of the chapters to your lives. The questions should promote a lively discussion when you gather. You will want to develop a companion notebook to keep with you while you study. Here you will write your journaled answers to the questions, any questions you have, and your assigned personal journaling.

I recommend that the group leader introduce the evening by reviewing the key points indicated at the end of the assigned chapter. He may want to emphasize a point that was especially significant to him. He could then open it up for others to share concepts that were revelation for them. From there you could discuss the questions as a group.

I pray that the group may intensify and quicken your learning experience, as your heart witnesses others walking the same path of deepened spiritual encounter. Blessings as you travel!

Chapter One

The Wretched Man Syndrome

I lay in bed, tossing and turning, not able to fall asleep. What if I died tonight? Would I go to heaven? No, I knew I wouldn't. I had attended my conservative Baptist church long enough to know that only those who had accepted Jesus into their hearts would make it to heaven. And I hadn't done that. No, I still wanted to go "my way." To give it all up for "His way" seemed just too much to ask. So I had resisted, year after year, knowing that if I died, I would be headed straight to hell.

The Night God Chased Me Down

But tonight was my night. God must have singled me out and said to His angels, "Go get that boy. I have need of him." Toss and turn as much as I would, I could not drop off to sleep. One thought ran constantly through my mind: "What if the house burns down tonight? I would go straight to hell." I could not shake it. I am sure it is because the angel kept whispering it into my ear.

So, finally, after a couple of hours of relentless angelic pressure,

I gave in, got up and went downstairs. My parents were at a church meeting, so I sat in a living room chair to make my announcement when they returned: I was giving my heart to Christ.

I was fifteen years of age when I was baptized and joined our conservative Baptist church. My repentance was thorough. My commitment was firm. Jesus was Lord of my life. I was heaven bond. Yippee! I felt the release within my spirit. I felt peace sweep over my soul. I knew I was born anew. I was a child of God.

Seeking Spiritual Growth and Sanctification

I had an immediate desire to saturate myself in the Word of God, which I did. A year later, I decided to commit my life full-time to the ministry. By age eighteen, I was enrolled at Roberts Wesleyan College near Rochester, New York, where I spent four years being trained for the pastoral ministry. I wanted to give God my all. I worked as a youth pastor for three of those years, and shortly after graduation was pastoring my own church.

Life was really starting to cook. I was preaching every Sunday, discovering from the Word of God new truths revealing how to please and serve God more effectively. Week after week I would share these with my congregation, teaching them how they could live more effectively for God. We studied holiness and righteousness, witnessing and prayer, and the need to love our enemies. I taught about giving and tithing and alms and becoming financially free. We organized witnessing teams and went door to door. We organized early morning prayer times and set aside days for fasting. I taught about becoming pure in heart, developing self worth, the principle of meekness, and developing God's priorities. We learned about putting off sins of the tongue, becoming like Jesus, pulling down strongholds. I taught a series on Christian living in the home, and how to establish proper eating habits. I taught about the believer and the Law, how to heal depression, the beatitudes, overcoming lust and adultery. The list went on and on.

The Load Became Heavy

Then something strange happened. One of my deacons sat down with me one day in my study and said, "Mark, I don't want to hear any more sermons. I can't even do all the things I know to do now, and if I hear any more, I will just feel even more guilt about all the additional ways I am failing God." I understood his problem. I was feeling it, too. It seemed that no matter how much I did for God, it was never enough. But what could I do? I was a preacher; I needed to preach. I couldn't stop preaching just because my frail flesh could not keep all the commands of God I was discovering in the Word.

No, I must preach. But something had to change. The load had become heavy. There were so many things to do if I was going to be a good Christian, it was impossible to remember them all. And when I would discover one which I had forgotten to do, I would instantly feel guilt and condemnation. Jesus had said His yoke was easy and His burden was light, but it certainly didn't feel very easy or light to me! I remembered that when I was first saved I had felt pretty light. However, as soon as I began to study what God expected of me, things became heavy in a hurry. Obviously, Jesus didn't understand that when you live in flesh as frail as mine, life is not as easy and light as it appeared to Him. Or was I messing up Christianity some way, making what was supposed to be easy and light very hard and difficult? I wondered.

The Wretched Man Syndrome

Not only was Christianity becoming heavy and burdensome for me because there were so many things to remember to do,

I also found that when I tried to do many of the things God wanted me to do, my flesh screamed in protest: "Make me!" I said, "You *will* do this..." and immediately we entered a knock-down, drag-out battle.

Take loving my enemies, for instance. Someone would attack me in some way (not understanding, of course, my greatness, love, devotion and purity!), coming against me with gossip and slander. My flesh would rise up and say, "All right, Mr. Perfect, you think you are so hot, let me tell you a thing or two!" Then the battle would begin. Reminding myself that the law of God said I was to love my enemies, I would put a smile on my face, set my will and say, "You will love this wretch, even if it kills you." Well, it usually killed me. My flesh would fight and storm and scream and howl and have a royal fit. But since God graced me with a strong will, it would finally prevail and, on the outside at least, I would say loving, kind words. Not that my insides felt all that loving. They were mostly dead, because I told them, "You will die to that anger you feel." As a result, eventually I was very, very dead on the inside, while on the outside I was smiling, saying loving words, and doing loving deeds. This didn't seem to be quite the way Christianity was supposed to work! As I recalled, I was supposed to feel love, joy, peace, and patience on the inside rather than simply anger and deadness.

Coming Face to Face with Will Worship

Then my wife complicated the situation even more. Patti said to me one day, "Christianity only works for those who have a strong will. It doesn't work for weak-willed people." You see, Patti's will appeared weaker than mine, and she was much more prone to giving in to doubt or depression or other negative emotions, rather than holding them inside and smashing them to bits as I was able to do. Her statement cut me to the quick. I knew that Christianity must be able to work for all, for those who had weaker wills as well as for those who were stronger.

Becoming Confused

Now I was confused, which is great, because I've learned that confusion is the first step toward revelation. Wasn't my approach to Christianity right? Could it be fundamentally flawed? I sure hoped not, because I had spent ten years as a Christian building this way. However, the end product of my life at this point seemed to be very similar to Paul's cry of frustration in Romans chapter seven.

> For what I am doing, I do not understand. For what I will to do, that I do not practice; but what I hate, that I do...Now if I do what I will not [to do], it is no longer I who do it, but sin that dwells in me. I find then a law, that evil is present with me, the one who wills to do good. For I delight in the law of God according to the inward man. But I see another law in my members, warring against the law of my mind, and bringing me into captivity to the law of sin which is in my members. O wretched man that I am! Who will deliver me from this body of death? (Rom. 7:15, 20-24)

That is exactly what I had come to, that same **wretched man syndrome.** At war with myself. Constantly trying to be good. Always trying to do the right thing. Feeling either inner war or inner deadness coupled with a lack of love, joy and peace. I knew there had to be more to Christianity than this. Was this the abundant life God talked about — man constantly struggling and at war internally with himself? If it is, it is rather hard to export. I could picture myself saying to a non-Christian, "You can accept Jesus as your Lord and Savior and become like me, full of inner war, guilt, tension, and condemnation." He would, of course, say, "No thanks, I have enough problems of my own." So I stopped witnessing because my experience was not worth passing on. And I said, "God, please teach me what I am doing wrong."

The Dawning Revelation of What Actually Happened at Salvation

God began bringing the right books, teachers, and experiences into my life and during the following months taught me seven truths which have set me free from guilt, condemnation, war, inner turmoil, and the Law. They are the following:

Truth # 1 — God Is All and In All

Truth # 2 — I Am a Vessel

Truth # 3 — I No Longer Live

Truth # 4 — Christ Is My Life

Truth # 5 — I Am Dead to the Law

Truth # 6 — I Live by the Spirit (*rhema* and *vision*)

Truth # 7 — I Live by Faith that God is Immanuel

In the following seven chapters we will examine what God taught me about each of the above seven truths which released the Divine power of Almighty God through the fusion of His Holy Spirit to my spirit.

Review of Key Points from Chapter One

☐ The salvation experience brings with it a sense of peace, joy and lightness.

☐ Often as one begins to study the Bible and see the commands of God for his life, a sense of heaviness returns as one finds it difficult to obey all the commands he is discovering.

☐ Often there is an inner war as one finds his flesh struggling against his spirit in an effort to be holy.

☐ This results in what Paul called the "wretched man syndrome."

☐ Add other ideas that were key points for you. Use your separate journal.

Think and Discuss

☐ Recall your own salvation experience. Take a few minutes to share it with your group. If anyone in the group has never had a salvation experience, ask if they would like to meet Jesus as their Lord and Savior. If so, lead them into salvation.

☐ Have you experienced the inner war and struggle discussed in this chapter? If so, share a bit of your experience with your group.

☐ Have you ever fallen into will worship, that is, a dependency on the strength of your will to accomplish things? Discuss this with the group. If we are not to set our will to come against sin, how are we supposed to use our will?

☐ Do you experience condemnation, or have you reached the place of no condemnation spoken of in Romans 8:1? If you experience condemnation in your life, what causes it? How is it possible to overcome it? By living a perfect life? What are the chances of that?

☐ Have you found a way out of the wretched man syndrome that Paul speaks of at the end of Romans chapter seven, or are you ensnared in the problem? If you have found a way out, describe the way in as much detail as possible to your group.

☐ **Journaling** — Write down this question in a separate journal: "Lord, what do You want to say to me about the truths of this chapter?" If you are unfamiliar with journaling as the author teaches it, read his book *Communion with God* or *Dialogue with God* which teaches this process in depth. (*Communion with God* has a more left brain, logical, outline style, while *Dialogue with God* is more right brain and story oriented). Journaling is simply the writing out of your prayers and God's answers, as David did in the Psalms. Record what God speaks to you by way of journaling in a special book. If it is not too personal, you may want to read some of it in your small group. That will be edifying and encouraging for all who hear, as well as confirm to you that it really is the Lord speaking to you, as the others in the group affirm the quality of your journaling. Make sure to begin every journal entry with a question written at the top of your blank sheet of paper. The simple act of writing the question often is the stimulus that precipitates your openness to receiving the response. See Appendix A for a brief overview of the four keys to hearing God's voice.

Chapter Two

Truth # 1 —
God Is All and in All

Yes, there is more to Christianity than the "wretched man syndrome" spoken of by Paul in Romans chapter seven. Paul himself describes the way out in Romans eight. We will try to follow his path in the next few chapters.

How Do We View God?

The first revelation that must burn in our hearts is the revelation of who God is. Is He a great Potentate in the sky? Is He an impersonal Being or is He interested in the most minute aspect of our lives? Does He view the world from a detached perspective, or is He intimately involved in its every function?

In my confused state, I used to think of God as One who had power and might and love and peace. I saw Him as One who had many attributes which I needed. I would often ask Him for these things, saying, "God, would you please give me..." I saw God as rather distant, and I would look up and call out to Him and beseech Him to come and meet me. I often felt separated from Him. He was over there, I was over here. He was up there, I was down here. He was the Holy One, I was the unholy one. I needed to be strengthened by Him.

Christian Humanism — I Live

Sometimes I would even forget to look to Him. I would use my own strength and my own might to accomplish those things which I felt I could handle. I thought, "Why bother God with such trivial things?" So even if I remembered to ask Him, sometimes I wouldn't, because He surely had more important things to do than trifle with this small item. Besides, He has given me the natural powers to do it myself. So I would just go ahead and live.

God began to break down these faulty notions and half-truths and reveal Himself to me in ways I had never seen before.

He Is Almighty God

The first observation He drove home to me was that He is Almighty God! That is something I had said for years but never really pondered. What does it mean that God is Almighty God? How much might does that give to Him? How much does that leave for me, for satan, for others? You guess! I decided that being Almighty must mean that He has all the might in the universe. That means if any might is expressed, it is an expression of the God who has all might. Not that God is the author of evil. That is a different problem, which we can discuss in a minute. No, what I am saying is that even the breath of the heathen who is cursing the name of Almighty God has been given to him by the hand of Almighty God. If God would remove His sustaining power, the heathen's life would immediately be snuffed out. God is all and in all.

If you claim to have all might, you must have all might, unless, of course, you are a liar. One thing I know is that God is not a liar. Therefore, if He says He has all might in the universe, then I believe He has all might.

However, God did not say He had all might, did He? Go back and read Genesis 17:1.

> When Abram was ninety-nine years old, the Lord appeared to Abram and said to him, "I am Almighty God; walk before Me and be blameless."

Does that say He has all might? I don't think so. What does it say? It says He **IS** all might. Is there a difference between **having** all the might in the universe and **being** all the might in the universe? If I have something, I can give it to you. If I *am something you want or need, then I must give myself to you.*

Not "Has" But "Is"

God does not **have** all might in the universe. He **is** all might in the universe. Therefore, if I am expressing might, Who am I expressing? You guessed it — God! If you are expressing might or power in your life, Who are you expressing? That's right, Almighty God, because all expression of might and power is an expression of Almighty God. When I raise my right arm, Whose strength is being expressed, mine or God's? Do I have any might or strength of my own? Not if God has all of it. Therefore, it is God's might that is being expressed.

If God *has might*, then I can ask Him to **give me some**, like a commodity. "I need this particular commodity. Lord, would you please provide it for me?" He can be there and I can be here, and He can hand me some of this thing I am asking for. However, if **God is all might** and I need might, then I must ask **Him to be present**, manifesting Himself in the situation. I will be saying, "God, I acknowledge You as Immanuel, God with me. I thank You that Your life and power are present and flowing in this situation. I speak forth a full release of the power and might of Almighty God over the situation before me." You may wonder why we have to call forth this release of the power and presence of God. The answer is that God has voluntarily limited Himself to the requests of His children (Ezek. 22:30,31) because He has us in training camp, learning how to win over the enemy and reign as kings and priests with Him in glory.

Even when individuals have chosen to utilize God's might and perform evil with it, is it still God's might? Are they still His servants? He is all and in all. For example, consider Nebuchadnezzar, the evil Hitler of the Old Testament, who went around destroying nations and taking them captive. Was he God's servant?

What About the Might of Evil Men?

In Jeremiah 25:9 God is speaking and says,

> "Behold, I will send and take all the families of the north," says the Lord, "and Nebuchadnezzar the king of Babylon, **My servant**, and will bring them against this land, against its inhabitants, and against these nations all around, and will utterly destroy them, and make them an astonishment, a hissing, and perpetual desolations."

Even the evil king Nebuchadnezzar was God's servant performing God's will. Did Nebuchadnezzar recognize himself as God's servant doing God's will? Not on your life! He thought he was **his own self-made man,** exercising his own wonderful power. Nebuchadnezzar could not look through the appearance of surface reality to true reality. Hear what he says:

> "By the strength of **my hand** I have done [it], and **by my wisdom,** for **I am prudent**; also **I have** removed the boundaries of the people, and have robbed their treasuries; so **I have** put down the inhabitants like a valiant [man]. **My hand** has found like a nest the riches of the people, and as one gathers eggs [that are] left, **I have**

gathered all the earth; and there was no one who
moved [his] wing, nor opened [his] mouth with even a
peep" (Isa. 10:13,14).

What Is God's Version of the Same Story?

Well now, God has a bit firmer grasp on reality so He sets the
record straight, responding to Nebuchadnezzar's arrogance by asking:

Shall the ax boast itself against him who chops with it?
[Or] shall the saw magnify itself against him who saws
with it? As if a rod could wield [itself] against those
who lift it up, [or] as if a staff could lift up, [as if it were]
not wood! Therefore, the Lord, the Lord of hosts, will
send leanness among his fat ones; and under his glory
he will kindle a burning like the burning of a fire
(Isa. 10:15,16).

God's version of reality is quite different from Nebuchadnezzar's. God believes that Nebuchadnezzar is simply an ax in His
hand, and doesn't think Nebuchadnezzar should be boasting at
all about it being **his strength** that has done any of these things.
Therefore, to help Nebuchadnezzar see, God is going to send
him some leanness of soul. How is that for a different version
of reality?

Now it is time to discover how firm a grasp on reality I have.
Do I see that all might is God in action, or do I see self and satan
and fate ruling this universe? Do I really believe He is King of
Kings and Lord of Lords, the Alpha and Omega, the Beginning
and the End, or do I think that "I" have my own strength, and
satan has his own strength? What do you see? How clear is your
grasp of reality?

The Problem of "Might" Being Used for Evil

Coming back to the question of "How can God be ruler over
evil?" I propose that we consider His title of King of Kings and

Lord of Lords. If God is really King over all the kings of this earth, and Lord over all the lords of this earth, is He not ruler over evil? Are not some of these kings evil kings? Are not some of these lords evil lords? If a man chooses to use the might of God within him in reverse, that is, to use it for evil rather than for good, does that make it any less God's might that is being used? Because man is trying to act on his own in reverse of God's plan for his life, does that mean God no longer has control over him?

I think of Joseph's brothers who were moved with jealousy, anger and envy to sell Joseph into Egypt. Was God no longer in control of their actions now that they were seeking to operate Almighty God's power in reverse and use the might of their right hand to destroy rather than to heal? What do you think?

Joseph was a seer. He was one who could see into the purposes of God, and when he looked to see, he saw that God still ruled, even when his brothers chose to use God's might within them in reverse. He said,

> But as for you, you meant evil against me; [but] God meant it for good, in order to bring it about as [it is] this day, to save many people alive (Gen. 50:20).

Do you see that deeply as you walk through life? Can you see that even the might of the evil man is the might of God in action, simply being used in reverse, yet still under God's control? How do you think one is able to see that deeply? Do we try to think that way? I don't believe so. My mind is not that expansive, my understanding that great. I would have a nervous breakdown if I thought I had to be that smart. Instead, I pray. I say, "God, would You please speak to me and show me what is going on?" And He begins speaking into my journal, granting me revelation and insight far beyond anything I have ever imagined or dreamed. Therefore, I do not become wise and expansive in mind and heart through striving to do so. I become wise and expansive by listening to the voice of the Wise and Expansive One within me. Much simpler, don't you think, than trying yourself to be godlike? Just let God be God within you. Relax into His arms. Cease from your own labors and enter into His rest (Hebrews 3 & 4).

For further contemplation, consider the situation of the angry mob shouting, "Crucify Him! Crucify Him!" and the spineless Pilate who would not stand up for righteousness. Then look at God's perspective of the entire day as recorded in Acts 4:27,28.

God Is Love

Here is another of God's attributes; or is it? Does the God we worship have love to give me, or is He Love? If I need love, and come asking Him to give me some, am I asking amiss or am I praying correctly? What do you think?

I believe I am asking amiss. I think such praying can easily rest on very large misunderstanding of who God is and who we are. Since we are not talking about **who we are** in this chapter, we will save that discussion until later. However, we are talking about **who God is**, so let's see what John says about Him.

> And we have known and believed the love that God has for us. **God is love**, and he who abides in love abides in God, and God in him (I John 4:16).

If I need love, do I need something God has, or do I need something God is? If I need something He has, I can ask Him for it. If I need something He is, then I need to ask **for Him** to be shed abroad in my heart through the Holy Spirit.

Not a Self Improvement Program, But a Replacement Program

You may be saying to yourself, "It's just a matter of words, you know, how you say it." NO, NO, NO! It is not just a matter of words. I would never fight over a word. My fight is to see that you have the experiences with the Holy Spirit that God has intended. The difference between the above two prayers is the difference between night and day, between Christianity and religion, between God and satan.

If you remember, it was satan who said, "You can be like God." He is the one who is constantly tempting me to establish in myself godlike characteristics. "You will be like God..." (Gen. 3:5), satan says. Pray hard and try hard to become that which you want to become or you think you should become. Try, try, try! The best response to those demonic thoughts is, "Go back where you came from!" because they came directly from the pit of hell.

If God is not after a self-improvement program in which I can work hard at becoming righteous and loving and knowing and everything else, then what kind of a program is God running? It is a replacement program in which He replaces myself with Himself, and I become hidden in Christ, who has become my Life. He does away with my self-consciousness and replaces it with a God-consciousness. A branch in a vine is not conscious of itself. It is conscious that it is a part of the vine, and that **its life flow streams continuously from the vine which is the core of its life.** We will talk more of this in a later chapter. Just let me say that we are not playing a game of mumble jumble with words. We are talking about two entirely different ways of living.

God is love, and when I need love, what I need is to experience the flow of God within me. It is that simple. So I ask Him to flow, fixing my eyes upon Him and tuning to the spontaneous River welling up within my heart. And sure enough, God flows out through my life. This is very different than fixing my eyes on myself and saying, "God help **me.**"

The Peace of God or the God of Peace

Now for another characteristic of God. God has peace. Or is He peace (Phil. 4:7,9)? I know that there are many times I need peace, and when I come to Him in my prayer time all disturbed, He speaks into my journal, "Mark, be at peace, I am here." He must have told me about a thousand times to be at peace because He was there, until finally I decided to be at peace because God was there. Theologically I knew that God was Immanuel, God with me. However, it is one thing to have a theological truth, and quite another to have a living experience. It was through experiencing God as a person, through the ongoing encounter of journaling, that I was finally pulled away from living in my theological truths and learned to live in and out of fellowship with the Holy Spirit (II Cor. 13:14).

Again, it was satan who tempted us all to live out of the tree of knowledge, to try to become like God ourselves, knowing good and evil. We tried living satan's way and we now have 2300 denominations that have each figured out right from wrong, and have established their camps around their knowledge. The 2300 camps pretty well prove we are doing something wrong, because Jesus said we were to be one. And the only way I know to be one is to quit eating from the tree that God forbade me to eat from, the tree of knowledge of good and evil (i.e., quit living in my mind), and begin instead to live out of the tree of life which, of course, is Him, Jesus the Vine and we the branches. I have learned to live out of the spontaneous flow of God within my heart which I record in my journal rather than out of my reasoning processes.

We will talk more about this in a later chapter. At this time, suffice it to say that we are not looking for a theology about who God is. We are looking for a flow of Almighty God within our hearts and spirits. Eventually it begins to dawn upon me that God is all and in all, and that Christ is my life.

Key Points from Chapter Two

☐ God is bigger than I thought.

☐ God is Almighty.

☐ God is Love.

☐ God is Peace.

☐ What I need is God.

☐ I don't need God to give me some of His attributes, I need Him to be my life.

☐ List in your journal other points that especially ministered to you.

Think and Discuss

☐ How do you see God? Has this chapter challenged the way you see Him? If so, how? Describe any transition you are going through.

☐ Have you been trained to eat from the tree of knowledge or the tree of life? How does one live out of the tree of knowledge? How does one live who lives out of the tree of life?

☐ Is journaling a regular activity in your life? Are you, like David and others in Scripture, able to write down the things God is speaking to you? Does it seem important for you to be able to do so? Would it fill any need you feel in your life?

☐ Do you live out of a theology about God, or an experience with Him? Which did the Pharisees live out of? Is it acceptable to live out of experience, or are we to live out of theology? (Those wanting a deeper understanding of this dilemma and a well-thought-out and practically supplied solution are referred to *Experiencing God* by the same author.)

☐ Meditate on the following verses in light of the truths of this chapter. You may want to write down your prayerful reflections in a separate notebook. Hebrews 11:3; Colossians 1:11,17; Acts 17:28; I Corinthians 1:30; Colossians 3:4.

☐ Concerning the theme of God as Almighty, read Isaiah 45:5-7 (and surrounding verses); Psalms 75:6,7; Proverbs 21:1; Romans 8:28; Romans 13:1-5; Ephesians 5:20; I Thessalonians 5:18.

☐ **Journaling** — Ask God what He wants to say to you about the truths of this chapter. Record what He says in a separate notebook (journal). (Be sure to write your question at the top of your page as a method of prompting your openness to Divine flow.) If it is not too private, come prepared to read your journaling in your small group. And thank you for being willing to share your heart with others. May God's richest blessings be upon you.

Chapter Three

Truth # 2 — I Am a Vessel

How do you view yourself? Are you strong, intelligent, wise, loving, caring, hospitable, courageous? Can you make up your own mind? Can you think things through clearly? Are you able to function effectively in life? Do you come to grips with the pressures around you in a mature way? Have you learned to handle them? How do you view yourself?

It took me a long time to comprehend who "I" was. For the longest time I thought "I" was quite something: rather intelligent, knowledgeable, strong; able to make my own decisions; able to think things through and arrive at wise decisions; able to initiate action when called upon to do so; able to pray for a friend when called upon; able to live my life; able to give my life; able to act.

I knew that before I gave my life to the Lord, I was one who had **gone my own way** (Isa. 53:6). However, now I intended to go God's way. I intended to live my life for Him. I was now going to serve Him, love Him, and worship Him. I went door to door witnessing because I wanted to tell others about Him. I set my will to overcome sin in my life, and to live holy before Him.

However, if you will notice, the word "I" is in the center of every phrase in the last paragraph. Not only is the word "I" there, the concept of "I" is even more powerfully there. **"I"** am the one doing.... I have the strength.... I have the smarts.... I have the will-power.... I have the might....

This whole mentality rests on a faulty understanding of who I am. I am not a package in myself. I am not complete in myself. I am not a self-contained unit. I am incomplete because I am hollow. **I am a vessel!**

A Vessel?

"A vessel?" you say.

> But we have this treasure in earthen vessels, that the excellence of the power may be of God and not of us (II Cor. 4:7).

Yes, a vessel! Now, I need to think about that for a minute. What is the sole purpose of a vessel? The only purpose of a vessel is to contain something. You mean the single reason I exist is to contain something? I just sit down and let myself be filled by something? Nah, I'm not into that. I'm not into looking afar off for some mystical or spiritual power or presence to flow through me. I like to show that **"I"** can stand on my own two feet, and what **"I"** can do with my own power. I can pray with my own mouth. I can love, I can hate, I can.... You name it, I can do it.

No, you just think you can because you have fallen for the deception that satan offered in the Garden of Eden, when he told Adam and Eve that rather than simply live from the tree of life, (i.e., out of Another), they could live out of themselves. "They" could know.... The emphasis was on **them**. **"You"** can be like God.... So Adam and Eve believed this deception and fell from God-consciousness to self-consciousness. Instead of seeing themselves as ones who lived out of fellowship with Another, that fellowship was broken, and they began living out of themselves. Now when God called to them, they hid. Divine fellowship was severed and self-consciousness was inaugurated.

Just maybe the step of salvation involves the step back from self-consciousness to God-consciousness. Maybe I am supposed to get over this ego trip that I am so great and wonderful and able and realize that I have been designed to contain something.

Containing Not Something, But Someone

However, I am not designed to contain simply "something"; I have been designed to contain Someone. I am not just a vessel, I am actually a temple...

> Or do you not know that your body is the temple of the Holy Spirit [who is] in you, whom you have from God, and you are not your own? (I Cor. 6:19)

What is the one purpose of a temple? May I suggest that it is to contain a god? And in this case, we have been designed to contain the God of this universe, God Almighty!

Someone Else Flows Through Us

Not only are we a temple that contains Almighty God, Christ has become a Vine and we are the branches...

> "I am the vine, you [are] the branches. He who abides in Me, and I in him, bears much fruit; for without Me you can do nothing" (John 15:5).

A temple may house a god, but a branch gets its very life from its vine. And this life is continuously, effortlessly there. Therefore, there is a continuous, effortless flow of Almighty God through my being that likely appears so natural I become totally unaware of it, and think, in my delusion, that it is me living.

However, it really isn't. It is the life flow of the "sap" from the vine.

I am more than a vessel containing a liquid, I am designed as a temple that houses the River of the Holy Spirit. God flows within me as a River...

> On the last day, that great [day] of the feast, Jesus stood and cried out, saying, "If anyone thirsts, let him come to Me and drink. He who believes in Me, as the Scripture has said, out of his heart will flow rivers of living water." But this He spoke concerning the Spirit, whom those believing in Him would receive; for the Holy Spirit was not yet [given], because Jesus was not yet glorified (John 7:37-39).

As I walk through life, I am not to think of myself as living alone, out of my own strength or abilities. No, I am one who walks tuned to the spontaneous River within my heart. I draw my strength and life out of that. I am delivered from self-consciousness to God-consciousness. I do not tune to my mind and my abilities. I tune to my heart and the stream of living water that flows from deep within. That is the Source of my power. That is the Source of my strength. When I need willpower, I turn to the One who lives within me and I fix my eyes upon Him, saying, "Jesus, be my Strength in this situation." I am not looking for Him to improve **me**. I am looking for Him to be me (i.e., my life in this situation, and in every situation). But we can even go one step beyond this.

An Organic Union

> And He is the head of the body, the church, who is the beginning, the first-born from the dead, that in all things He may have the pre-eminence (Col. 1:18).

Just as it is the head that gives all commands to the body, so it is Jesus who gives all commands to me. I live constantly with my eyes on Him (Heb. 12:1), tuned to the Divine initiative, watching His vision, hearing His words, and acting them out. I live just as He did as He walked this earth...

> Then Jesus answered and said to them, "Most assuredly, I say to you, the Son can do nothing of Himself, but what He sees the Father do; for whatever He does, the Son also does in like manner" (John 5:19).

> I can of Myself do nothing. As I hear, I judge; and My judgment is righteous, because I do not seek My own will but the will of the Father who sent Me (John 5:30).

This, then, is how I am to live life. Life is not me doing anything on my own initiative. It is not me trying to love, or me trying to live, or me trying to pray. No, I am one who is joined to Another (I Cor. 6:17). He is my Life. He is my Strength. He guides my thoughts. I do nothing on my own initiative. When I need to know how to think about a certain thing, I tune to the spontaneous flow bubbling up from my heart and fix my eyes on Jesus, saying, "Lord, would You give me Your perspective on this situation, so I know how to perceive it?" And sure enough, spontaneously, effortlessly, a flow of pictures, thoughts and feelings begins welling up within me as the River of the Holy Spirit manifests its flow within me.

I Didn't See This Clearly When I First Accepted Christ

When I gave my life to the Lord Jesus Christ, I did not realize that I was a container for Another. No, sir, I thought "I" had been living my life all these years. I did not realize that before salvation, I was still obviously a container. However, then I lived out of the spirit of this world rather than the Divine Spirit. I had not yet opened my heart to the One who is All and in all, so even though He was available to me, and even though He was giving me the life and breath I was using to curse His name, I did not recognize Him. I thought He was far away — off in heaven somewhere, very distant from my life. I had not acknowledged Him as Lord. I thought I was lord, that I ran my own life, that I did my own thing.

How foolish and nearsighted! I was simply controlled by another spirit, the spirit of this world, and was by nature a child of wrath.

> And you [He made alive], who were dead in trespasses and sins, in which you once walked according to the course of this world, according to the prince of the power of the air, **the spirit who now works in the sons of disobedience**, among whom also we all once conducted ourselves in the lusts of our flesh, fulfilling the desires of the flesh and of the mind, **and were by nature children of wrath**, just as the others (Eph. 2:1-3).

I was not my own boss, doing my own thing. I was under satan's command and I was doing his thing.

> But God be thanked that [though] you were **slaves of sin,** yet you obeyed from the heart that form of doctrine to which you were delivered. And having been set free from sin, you became **slaves of righteousness** (Rom. 6:17,18).

I have always been someone's slave. Either I was controlled by the spirit which now works in the sons of disobedience, and I was a slave of sin, or I am indwelt by the Divine Spirit and have become a slave of His power. I am one who is controlled or indwelt by another.

> By which have been given to us exceedingly great and precious promises, that through these you may be **partakers of the divine nature**, having escaped the corruption [that is] in the world through lust (II Pet.1:4).

There you have it. We are either controlled by the spirit of this world or we are containers of the Divine Spirit. This results in our being either a slave of sin or a slave of righteousness. In either case, we are not our own boss.

Review of Key Points from Chapter Three

- [ ] We are vessels.
- [ ] We are temples.
- [ ] We are branches grafted into a Vine.
- [ ] We are Christ's body and He is the head.
- [ ] We only live out of Divine initiative.
- [ ] Even before we were saved we were vessels.
- [ ] Before salvation, we were slaves to the spirit of this world. Now we contain the Divine Spirit.
- [ ] List other points that are especially helpful or significant to you from this chapter.

Think and Discuss

- [ ] Is even satan a vessel (Isa. 14:12-15; Ezek.28:11-17)? (The name *Lucifer* means "light-bearer.")
- [ ] Were you conscious of the fact that you were a vessel before you came to Christ? How did you think of yourself?
- [ ] Do you live out of a consciousness of the fact that you are a vessel now that you have come to Christ? Do you live only out of Divine initiative? Describe your experience as you walk through a day. Do you plan it, or do you look to God to plan it? Do you talk to God about it, or are your actions self-initiated? Do you look to your wisdom, or do you tune to the intuitive voice of your spirit and the Holy Spirit joined to your spirit? Do you look to your strength, or do you abandon yourself to the might of Almighty God?
- [ ] What is the best way to remain conscious of the fact that we are vessels, or temples or Christ's body? It seems so easy to

forget this and think of ourselves as self-contained units. Why do we forget this so easily? Why do we so readily fall back into the idea of ourselves as independent? Can we do anything to help prevent this? If so, what?

☐ Do you agree that the sin in the Garden of Eden resulted in a fall from God-consciousness to self-consciousness? If so, what is the most likely solution for self-consciousness, sin-consciousness and inferiority? Do you live most of your day as a self-conscious person or a God-conscious person? Describe your daily experience.

☐ **Journaling** — Spend some time journaling about the truths of this chapter. At the top of your page ask the Lord what He wants to say to you concerning your being a vessel. Record His response. Come prepared to read this to your small group. Encourage others as they hear the words which the Lord is speaking in your journal.

Chapter Four

Truth # 3 —
I No Longer Live

I needed a revelation of the truth discussed in the last chapter, that I am simply a container. I grew up as a heathen under the delusion that I was my own boss, that I did what I wanted, that I was a self-contained unit. I had no understanding that I was actually being bossed around by satan. I would say, "Nobody tells me what to do!" Want to bet? Satan did. His spirit, also, flows so easily and effortlessly through the human vessel that most people are unaware of his presence, and so they think it is themselves living life when in actuality it is satan expressing his life through them. They think they are their own bosses, when actually they are under satan's command. They think they are nobody's slave, when in reality, they are slaves of sin (Rom. 6:17).

The problem arose when I became a Christian. I carried my delusion right into my Christian life. Since I had believed that my pre-Christ days were me living for myself, I decided that in my post-Christ era I would live for Christ. But do you see the delusion? It was not me living independently in my pre-Christ days. Nor is it me living in my post-Christ days. Now it is Christ living through me.

> I have been crucified with Christ; it is no longer I who live... (Gal. 2:20).

Do you think I could understand the above verse? Not on your life! Oh, yes, I could quote it. I had some limited understanding as to what it may have meant theologically, but practically living it out was a totally different matter. I thought it meant that I was no longer to live for myself, but now I was to live for Christ. But you see that the crux of my thinking was that I was living as an autonomous individual. How totally devoid of reality! But that's the way I saw it. The illusion was just too great, and had been lived for too long.

For fifteen years I had thought that "I" lived life as an autonomous individual. I had no grasp of the reality that I was a container enslaved by another. I believed I was in charge. How foolish, now that I look back on it. But it wasn't foolish then. It was the only form of reality I knew. And no one was telling me anything different.

The Mixture of Christianity and Religion

My church was telling me that now "I" was to live for Christ, rather than telling me that Christ was to be my life. So I obediently followed the path of delusion, and tried to live for Christ. "I" would witness, rather than having Christ speak through me in an unpremeditated, spontaneous flow. My witnessing was a system of truths rather than an encounter with Divine power. Jesus didn't have a memorized spiel He used on heathen. He was simply a Container of Divine power which would be released though His life as He did only what He saw the Father doing and spoke only the words He heard the Father saying. He would heal the sick and raise the dead and cleanse the lepers, and evangelism would follow in the wake. How different than my puny attempts at evangelism! I would simply spew forth my memorized formulas, usually confronting, offending and driving away the sinner. Sinners did not flock to me to see the power of God, they fled from me so they would not be theologically pelted.

I would try to love, because good Christians are supposed to love their enemies. However, it was "I" in the center of the activity. "I am trying." The Bible very clearly says I am supposed to cease from all my trying and efforts and enter His rest (Heb. 3,4). So now that I know that I no longer live, I simply come to Christ, saying, "You are my Life, and You are the Love of this universe, so release Your love through this vessel at this time, I pray." You see, I am not talking about me at all anymore. I am not trying to get God to improve me. I am not fixing my eyes on me, or my needs or my anything, because I no longer live. Christ lives. Therefore, I fix my eyes on Christ who is my life and begin to call Him forth to release His life and manifest His supernatural power through this vessel which is His body. A totally different grasp of reality. A totally different perspective on life. It is the only perspective that works, I promise you. I think I have tried them all. This is the only thing that works in life for me.

Needed: A Deeper Understanding of the New Testament Commands

I needed a deeper understanding of the commands given in the New Testament. For example, Paul said,

> But fornication and all uncleanness or covetousness, let it not even be named among you, as is fitting for saints (Eph. 5:3).

I took that to mean that I was to put away fornication and all uncleanness. And again the emphasis was always on the active working of self rather than on resting in the Divine power that filled me.

There were so many commands in the New Testament. Some even said "I" was to carry them out. However, what I failed to realize was that the New Testament redefines "I."

The Redefined "I"

> I have been crucified with Christ; it is no longer I who live, but Christ lives in me; and the [life] which I now live in the flesh I live by faith in the Son of God, who loved me and gave Himself for me (Gal. 2:20).

Who is this new "I" the New Testament speaks of? It is no longer the self I; it is the "Christ I." Therefore, when the New Testament says "I" am to do something, what it means is that the "Christ I" is to do it, or that I am to let Christ do it through me. Therefore, I need to become very conscious of the redefined I. When I think of "I," I must think of "Christ I." When I live, I must be conscious that it is the "Christ I" living.

Again, when Paul says, "I can do all things through Christ who strengthens me" (Phil. 4:13), he is talking about the redefined I, the Christ I.

I can beat myself and say, "Self, now don't forget to think of yourself in this way from now on," which, of course, would be falling straight back into religion, because it is religion that says, "Self, do this" and "Self, do that." No, instead, I say, "Christ, please remind me of this truth any time I fall back into a self-consciousness and think it is simply me living life." Now the responsibility rests on the indwelling power of Almighty God to make you who you are, rather than on self trying to keep itself where it thinks it should be.

Religion, the "I Will Try to Do It" Syndrome

This whole religious syndrome is so insidious. It creeps in everywhere, all the time. Only Christ can heal it. The deception of being religious in your following of God is that it appears so right and looks so good from the outside, it is hard to believe it could actually be wrong or, even worse, demonic. But hear what the New Testament says about missing Christ, who is the head, and who is the power of our lives and instead following commands and rules which you try to obey.

> Let no one defraud you of your reward,...and not holding fast to the Head, from whom all the body, nourished and knit together by joints and ligaments, grows with the increase [which is] from God. Therefore, if you died with Christ from the basic principles of the world, why, as [though] living in the world, do you subject yourselves to regulations; "Do not touch, do not taste, do not handle," which all concern things which perish with the using — according to the commandments and doctrines of men? These things indeed have an appearance of wisdom in self-imposed religion, [false] humility, and neglect of the body, [but are] of no value against the indulgence of the flesh (Col. 2:18-23).

The bottom line is that I cannot do anything because I no longer live. I cannot love — it is God's love that is shed abroad in my heart. I cannot pray because I do not know how to, but the Spirit makes intercession with groanings too deep for words. I simply cling to the Head, whence all my strength comes. I do nothing on my own initiative, but only what I see, and only what I hear (John 5:19,20,30). Therefore, I am one who tunes to the Divine initiative as I walk through life. I look for God's vision to flow within my heart. I listen for God's words to be spoken within my heart. I record what He is saying and revealing, and I let Him do that great work that He has revealed though me. He has become the Alpha and the Omega, the beginning and the end. He is all and in all. He is my life.

A Review of Some Key Thoughts from Chapter Four

☐ I no longer live.

☐ I tend not to understand that I don't live.

☐ Religion doesn't understand that we don't live.

☐ Religion encourages us to strive, to try.

☐ Christianity commands us to ceasing striving and enter His rest.

☐ List other points that are especially important to you.

Think and Discuss

☐ Do you think of yourself in terms of the "self I" or the "Christ I"? Describe your mental and inner processes as they relate to this question.

☐ Have you been trained by religion to strive or by true Christianity to cease striving? Describe your learning. If you have been taught to strive, repent for accepting that lie, and renounce it as demonic so you can be freed to go on to a new life in Christ. In your small group you may want to spend time in prayer together.

☐ Journaling — "Lord, what do You want to say to me concerning the fact that I no longer live? Have I been caught up in religion? How can I be freed?" Record these questions and the Lord's answers in another notebook or journal. Come prepared to share your heart with your small group. It is always best if you can actually read a section of your journaling.

Chapter Five

Truth # 4 —
Christ Is My Life

We have finally gotten rid of self. He is no longer living for evil, nor is he living for good. He is no longer living at all. We are thoroughly prepared for God's replacement program. We have overcome the idea that this is some kind of a self-improvement plan in which God is going to make me better. No, not at all. He is going to do away with me entirely (that is, my experience of living as a self-conscious individual), and He is going to restore me to the experience of Eden, where I will live out of Divine fellowship and eat from the tree of life. No longer will I look to my knowledge, for that tree is forbidden. Now I will tune to my heart, to the flow that wells up within me as I fix my eyes on Jesus, the Author and Finisher of my faith. Now I do nothing on my own initiative. I have learned to live as Jesus the Pattern Son, who did nothing on His own initiative, but only what He heard and saw the Father doing (John 5:19,20,30).

However, it is going to take awhile to learn to live this way, because I have been so perfectly tutored in the wrong way. I have many habits, ingrained for years, that I will have to break. Did I say "I" will have to break them? Oh well, you see what I mean. It takes years to overcome the delusion. Let me try again. "I have many habits, ingrained for years, which **Christ** will have to break."

There, that is better. I am sure what I really need is a support group that helps me catch all these slip-ups so we can all more speedily arrive at our goal of "being in Christ, who is our life."

You may be wondering, "If 'I' am no longer engaged in doing all these tasks, what am 'I' supposed to be doing?" Great question! I hoped you would ask that.

The Function of the Human Vessel Is to Fix Itself upon Jesus

"I" am fixing my eyes on Jesus, the Author and Finisher of my faith. What exactly does that mean? In the Greek, the phrase "fixing our eyes" from Hebrews 12:1 literally means "to see distinctly to the exclusion of all else." That is not a bad place to start. That means I begin to see Christ everywhere I look. Of course, the Bible says when I give a loaf of bread to a hungry person I have given it to Christ, and when I give water to a thirsty person I have given it to Christ. That is true because Christ is all and in all. In Him all things hold together (Col. 1:17). That allows Him to express Himself through every atom of this universe.

I tune to vision as I walk through life and I say, "Lord, will You show me Yourself in this situation?" And in every single situation I become a seer. As the prophets of old, we see Him in the whirlwind, the storm, the hills, the trees, the creation, the child. David said, "Even if I go to hades You are there," so there is no place I can look and not see Immanuel, God with us.

While looking at the vision He places before my eyes, I ask Him to speak to me, and I tune to the spontaneous flow of thoughts, ideas and feelings that begin to bubble up within my heart. Now I have discovered the "Spirit of life in Christ Jesus" that Paul talked about in Romans eight.

So how do I live? I live as a receiver. I receive Divine input and then I live it out. Yes, activity does come, but only as a by-product of receptivity. The Lord told the Israelites,

> "I [am] the Lord your God, who brought you out of the land of Egypt; Open your mouth wide, and I will fill it" (Ps. 81:10).

Do you see the relationship? God is the mighty Deliverer. He is the power and might. I am the one who opens my mouth wide and lets God fill it. Have you ever seen a baby bird in the nest when the mother comes with worms? All you see is wide open mouths. That is our posture. We sit with wide open mouths receiving everything from God, and then letting Him live out through us any action He wants. And each action is done through the working of His might. If I do it through the working of my might, it becomes a dead work (Heb. 6:1,2).

Let Us Not Create "Ishmaels"

Do you remember when God told Abram what great things He was going to do through him (Genesis 12 & 15)? After waiting a while (eleven years) for God to do it, and seeing that God wasn't able without his help, Abram and his wife came up with a good idea of how to help God accomplish His purposes. Their efforts resulted in Ishmael, whom God rejected, saying, "No, I will give you a son through Sarai...." In the same way, I create Ishmaels whenever I rush ahead, trying to carry out God's word myself, through my strength, and in my wisdom. Most of my early Christian life was composed of Ishmaels, me trying to please God through my efforts.

Dead Works

God also calls these efforts "dead works."

> Therefore, leaving the discussion of the elementary
> [principles] of Christ, let us go on to perfection, not
> laying again the foundation of repentance from dead
> works and of faith toward God (Heb. 6:1).

A dead work is anything "I" do, rather than letting it flow out
of the Divine initiative (i.e., vision, *rhema*, burden and power).
Almost all of my early Christian life was dead works. It was me
in action. I was totally consumed by religion and phariseeism
and didn't even know it. The tragedy is that much of what passes
for Christianity today is caught in this same trap, because we
have been taught to eat from the "tree of knowledge" and not
to trust the "tree of life" (i.e., the intuitive and visionary flow
from our spirits).

"The kingdom of God suffers violence and violent men take
it by force." I am convinced that only those who will become
violent in their attack against this prevalent error in our culture
and our religious experience will actually enter into the fulness
of what God has prepared for them. Will you become one of
these violent ones? Will you come to the living Christ within
you for all of life, or will you settle for Him being a theological
concept? The choice is yours.

A New Way of Living

Now my prayers are similar to the following: "God, what was
that point You wanted to make? What was that name I forgot?
Break the power of the attack against me. Send an angel with
Your message to this person. Lord, remind me to.... Thank
You, Lord, for bringing that thought to my attention. Release
Your power through me right now. Lord, I release Your love
through me right now. Let Your love expand within my heart.
Circumcise my heart, cut out that anger and fear. I come against

the spirit of fear in the name of Jesus. I rebuke that negative thought in the name of Jesus. Lord, grant clarity of heart and mind. Lord, change the desires within my heart. Place Your desires there. Lord, I thank You that You have joined Yourself to me, and that You are my Life. I thank You that You are all the might in the world. Lord, please release Your power through me right now...."

We become conscious of our lives in and out of Another. We set our minds on things above, not on things that are on this earth, for we are dead and our lives are hidden with Christ in God.

Some Key Points from Chapter Five

☐ I no longer live for evil.

☐ I no longer live for good.

☐ I no longer live.

☐ Christ is my Life.

☐ I am not to strive to do things.

☐ I am to fix myself on Jesus only, always.

☐ Any work I do from my own initiative and in my own strength is a dead work of which I must repent.

☐ Any effort I make to fulfill God's visions for my life ends up creating Ishmaels, which cause many problems and are rejected by God. I must repent for all Ishmaels.

☐ Now my prayers are to call Christ forth.

☐ List other points that were especially meaningful to you.

Think and Discuss

☐ Does it make life too simple to simply fix yourself upon Christ? Aren't there other things we are supposed to fix ourselves upon also? What about fixing ourselves upon the activity before us? How can we fix ourselves upon Christ **and** upon the activity before us at the same time? Is that possible? If so, how? Describe how you do it. Is this what God wants?

☐ Is it possible to live in God-consciousness all the time? If so, describe how you have done it — even if only for a day. Is living in God-consciousness a habit we can learn? Can this habit replace the habit of living in self-consciousness? How long would it take to learn this new habit if we focused ourselves upon it? How long would it take to learn this new habit if we asked Christ to establish it within our hearts? Is it worth this amount of time? Will you commit yourself to learning this new way of living? Will you get with a group who will encourage you in the establishment of this new way of living? Will you encourage others in this group? If so, watch and be amazed at what God does in your life and in your group.

☐ List as many loving, kind ways as come to your mind that you could use to encourage yourself and others to move from self to Christ, when you see yourself (or them) walking in the illusion of self. (i.e. "Let's take a minute and quiet ourselves before Christ and see what He is saying about this." or "Let's take a minute right now and pray for God's power to be poured out over this situation.")

☐ **Journaling** — Take your journal and write on the top of the page, "Lord, what do You want to say to me concerning being my Life? What does it mean specifically and practically? Speak to me, I pray. Thank you, Lord." Then tune to spontaneity, fix your eyes on Jesus and write what flows within. Come prepared to share what you have written with your small group.

Chapter Six

Truth # 5 —
I Am Dead to the Law

To recap before going on: The way out of the "wretched man syndrome" is to realize that God is all and in all, and that we are simply vessels to be filled by Him. We don't live for ourselves, but Christ lives His life out through us. Can you believe that is all we have said so far? It sure has taken me a lot of pages to say that! Now, let us go on and explore another key that sets us free from the "wretched man syndrome."

I Used to Live with My Eyes Fixed on the Laws of God

I described this syndrome in Chapter One. I would see a command in the New Testament that I should do something, and I would try my best to obey that command. Then I would find another command, and try my best to obey that command also. Eventually I had so many commands I was juggling that the load became heavy. I felt guilt and accusation and condemnation and frustration, and cried, "This is not the abundant life!" Of course, the Lord agreed with me. This was not the abundant life! But what was I doing wrong? Wasn't I supposed to be fixing my eyes on the laws of God and trying to obey them?

You already know part of the answer. You already know that **you** don't try to do anything, but that you go to Christ and ask Him to move within you. You also know that **you don't live but Christ is your Life.** Now we are going to learn what place Law does have in the believer's life.

Preaching Mount Sinai or Mount Calvary

It was Paul Yonggi Cho who said, "You can either preach from Mount Sinai or from Mount Calvary." If you preach Mount Sinai, you preach about the laws of God. If you preach Mount Calvary, you preach about the power of the resurrected Christ within the heart of the believer. One leads to death and the other leads to life.

> [God]...also made us sufficient as ministers of the new covenant, not of the letter but of the Spirit; for the letter kills, but the Spirit gives life. But if the ministry of death, written [and] engraved on stones, was glorious, so that the children of Israel could not look steadily at the face of Moses because of the glory of his countenance, which [glory] was passing away, how will the ministry of the Spirit not be more glorious? For if the ministry of condemnation [had] glory, the ministry of righteousness exceeds much more in glory (II Cor. 3:6-9).

The Ministry of Condemnation and Death, or the Ministry of Righteousness and Life

Can you imagine having the "ministry of condemnation?" How about the "ministry of death?" You could be a traveling preacher, spreading condemnation and death everywhere you went. You could even have it written up in your promotional material:

"A specialist in the ministry of condemnation and death! I guarantee to bring guilt and condemnation into your life, because you deserve it. You have sinned, and God hates sinners. I will bring you face to face with the laws of God which you are breaking, so you can repent and come before Him in weeping and mourning. By the end of my sermon, you will be howling and moaning in your misery!"

Sounds inviting, doesn't it? Especially if I am already laboring under some unresolved guilt, and feel God probably "has it in" for me. "Come on, Mister Preacher, hit me again! I deserve it. Ahh, that feels good. Come on, one more time. Harder. Ahhh!"

Unfortunately, religion caters to this kind of sickness, which is why it becomes the laughingstock of the world. The minister of condemnation is preaching from Mount Sinai.

The other kind of ministry that is mentioned is the ministry of righteousness, the ministry of Spirit life. This preacher's promotional literature may read as follows:

"Let me tell you who you are in Christ. Christ has set you free from the Law and its attending guilt and condemnation, and has clothed you with a righteousness that is not your own, a righteousness that comes by faith. I will show you how to turn to Him, allowing all that God is to flow effortlessly and naturally through you. Come and learn that you no longer have any limits in your life except the limits of the Almighty Limitless God."

I hope you were drawn to this second speaker. He is preaching Mount Calvary. He is presenting New Covenant reality.

We Are Dead to the Law

Therefore, my brethren, **you also have become dead to the law through the body of Christ, that you may be married to another, [even] to Him who was raised**

from the dead, that we should bear fruit to God. For when we were in the flesh, the passions of sins which were aroused by the law were at work in our members to bear fruit to death. But now we have been delivered from the law, having died to what we were held by, so that we should **serve in the newness of the Spirit** and not [in] the oldness of the letter (Rom. 7:4-6).

Sometime during my life I must come to grips with the fact that I no longer live before the Law. That is, I no longer live with my attention fixed on the Law. People did that in the Old Covenant, but no longer. I have died and my life is hidden with Christ in God. Christ has completely satisfied the requirements of the Law, which I as a weak and sinful man was not able to do. Now Christ lives within me, empowering me to live a far more holy life than even the Law demands, if I will only fix my eyes on His inworking power. Of course, if I do not fix my eyes on Jesus and on His power as I walk through life, then indeed I may fall into sin. That is why I want to maintain the Law as a safety net under me, so if I do stop drawing from the life of the Spirit within me, I will only fall as far as the Law, and it will catch me so I do not fall into total disgrace and degradation.

The Purposes of the Law

What was the purpose of the Law? There were several. The Law was not part of God's initial design. It was **added because of transgression.** When I took my eyes off God, and broke my fellowship with Him in the Garden of Eden, God had to **add** law as a safety net to keep me from totally destroying myself. It kept me in custody so I would not self-destruct before the grace of Christ appeared in my life. If I didn't at least maintain the minimum requirements set down by the Law, I would destroy my life and not even be around to experience the beauty of God's grace in salvation.

> But before faith came, we were **kept under guard by the law,** kept for the faith which would afterward be revealed (Gal. 3:23).

So God added the Law to keep me from destroying myself. Also, the law was supposed to teach me something. It was a tutor with a specific lesson to teach: we could not in our own strength become perfect. There is none righteous, no not one. So I was to learn that even if I kept all the Law, I would still not arrive at the perfection that is in Christ.

> Therefore the law was our tutor [to bring us] to Christ, that we might be justified by faith. But after faith has come, we are no longer under a tutor (Gal. 3:24,25).

Did I learn my lesson when I came to Christ? That is, did I learn that I am to turn my gaze from the Law to Christ? No. I just tried even harder to discover all the laws within the Bible, and I focused on trying to keep them so I could please my Lord. Of course, the result was frustration, condemnation and death, because the end of the Law is death.

I had found Christ with my words (He is my Lord and Savior), but I had not yet found the road of faith.

> For you are all sons of God through faith in Christ Jesus. For as many of you as were baptized into Christ have put on Christ (Gal. 3:26,27).

I had no comprehension of putting on Christ, or of being in Christ, or of fixing my eyes on Christ as I walked through life. Instead I fixed my eyes on the Law, and the things I should be doing and discovered that, sure enough, the Law produced death in my life in the forms of guilt, condemnation, accusation, depression and eventually death. Not exactly the abundant life I had hoped for or been told about!

God Has Always Offered Fellowship — Man Has Chosen Law

God never intended that there be law in the first place. He had to add it because of the problem of broken fellowship and the resulting sin (Gal. 3:17,19). Even when He added it, He didn't desire it. Moses recounts the story in Deuteronomy five, and there you will see that God was actually offering the Israelites His voice! Restored fellowship! Restoration to the status of the Garden of Eden! But they turned Him down, because they didn't like the fire that came with His voice. As a result, God was forced to give them law instead.

Now God offers to the Church His voice one more time as He takes up residence within our hearts and brings us to a new mount, Mount Zion. The last mountain was Mount Sinai, the place of Law. This is Mount Zion, where we actually experience fellowship with the Holy Spirit. And He has only one caution:

See that you do not refuse Him who speaks (Heb. 12:25).

The worst possible response would be for me to turn my back on fellowship with God one more time and go back to living law. He has always wanted fellowship, from the Garden of Eden in Genesis to the ultimate marriage of the Bride in Revelation. He has always wanted fellowship with His creation. And we have generally turned Him down and eaten instead from the tree of the knowledge of good and evil while looking to our own efforts to either save us or to keep the laws once we have been saved.

Your Response

What will you do? Will you live out of law, trying to obey it, trusting it to provide safety? Or will you live out of the voice and vision of the Creator of this universe, Almighty God? Will you fix your eyes on the laws of the Word of God, or will you discover the Person of Christ Jesus on every single page as you read? Will you see yourself striving to keep the Law, or look within to the One who has already kept all the laws and now empowers you to far supersede them all?

You must choose. Either you will walk in fellowship with the Holy Spirit, sensing continuously the voice, vision and burden of God, being led by the Divine initiative, or you will live out of yourself and the laws you have discovered and are seeking to obey. One way results in life, the other in death. "Choose ye this day whom you will serve." If it be God, serve Him. If it be religion, serve it. However, know that it was religion that destroyed the Son of God in the midst of the sons of Israel.

I choose to live out of my relationship with God. I choose to look for vision constantly, to listen for His voice continually, and to believe that is more trustworthy than the reasonings of my mind. To make this choice I must step outside all the culture and training of my youth and childhood. It has not been an easy decision, but it has taken me places I would never have gone, and has released God's blessing in my life in ways I could never have imagined. God has led me on tours worldwide, sharing these truths with the body of Christ, while I had planned on being a dairy farmer in Lowville, New York. Isn't that just the way God is?

Will you join me in my decision to live out of fellowship with the Holy Spirit rather than legalism and law? I pray that you do.

Review of Some Key Points from Chapter Six

☐ We are dead to the Law.

☐ Law was never part of God's initial design.

☐ It was added later because of broken fellowship and sin.

☐ Restored fellowship removes the need for law once again. Law's temporary purposes include: a. To keep me from destroying myself before I discover God's grace working within my life. b. To teach me that I do not have the power to become perfect through keeping it. I need Christ's supernatural strengthening on a daily basis as I walk through life.

☐ God has always offered man fellowship.

☐ Man almost always refuses relationship and chooses law instead, breaking God's heart, while becoming a destructive legalist who persecutes those who have found the Spirit.

☐ Will you take the valiant step of embracing and trusting fellowship with God's Holy Spirit as you walk through life, maintaining the Law only as a safety net to keep you if you fall from grace?

☐ List other points that are especially important to you.

Think and Discuss

☐ What do you see as the purposes and value of the Law? What purposes has the Law filled in your life? In what ways has it helped you?

☐ What do you see as the limitations of the Law? In what ways has it hurt you as you have walked through life?

☐ Do you currently tend to focus on law as you walk through life, or do you tend to focus on the overcoming power of the One who lives within you? If your focus is not on Christ and the Spirit as you walk through life, why isn't it? What is keeping you from that focus? What would have to change within you for this focus to be realized? Will you make these changes now?

☐ Do you agree that both biblically and historically the legalists have resisted the prophets (i.e. those who live by law resist those who live by Spirit)? Which side of this fence have you been on? If you have not been on the side that God is on, do you want to make a change? If so, spend time in prayer and reorientation, asking God to transform you from within.

☐ **Journaling** — "Lord, what do You want to say to me about the place of the Law in my life?"

Chapter Seven

Truth # 6 —
I Live by the Spirit
(*Rhema* and Vision)

Great! I no longer must live under the Law. That is a relief, because I had trouble obeying it anyway. But now I am afraid. What is going to keep me from sinning and totally destroying my life and the lives of those around me?

First, it is important that we never throw the Law away. It always remains as a safety net under us. If we ever fall out of the Spirit, we still have the Law to catch and stabilize us while we get ourselves back into the Spirit, for we know that those who are led by the Spirit are not under the Law.

The second part of the answer is found in Romans 8:1,2:

[There is] therefore now no condemnation to those who are in Christ Jesus, who do not walk according to the flesh, but according to the Spirit. For the law of the Spirit of life in Christ Jesus has made me free from the law of sin and death (Rom. 8:1,2).

No condemnation! That's great. Because I have discovered that I live in Christ Jesus, I recognize that I no longer live, but He is now my life. We talked at length about this "Christ I," so that is pretty clear. But what is the new law verse two talks about, the **Law of the Spirit of life in Christ Jesus**? Can we explore this law a little bit so we see what it is and how it works?

The Law of the Spirit of Life in Christ Jesus

This must be one of the greatest laws in the Bible because it sets me free from the law of sin and death, and from the wretched man syndrome we spoke about in Chapter One. It is the law that heals the inner war within the heart and brings you to peace and power and love and no condemnation. That sounds great, Paul! What is this law?

Paul begins to work through a definition of this law in the first twelve verses of Romans eight. According to verse three, it **solves the problem of weak human flesh** which is not able to keep the Law. In verse four, God says He is going to make us able to meet the requirements of the Law, not by our striving with our own fleshly strength to do so, but **by the power of the Holy Spirit which resides within us!**

If I set my mind on the strength of my flesh to overcome the lusts of my flesh, I am hopelessly entangled in the wretched man syndrome, because my flesh is only as powerful as the other part of my flesh that I am fighting against. So I end up in a stalemate.

> For those who live according to the flesh set their minds on the things of the flesh, but those [who live] according to the Spirit, the things of the Spirit. For to be carnally minded [is] death, but to be spiritually minded [is] life and peace (Rom. 8:5,6).

The only solution is to **set my focus on the power of the Spirit of God that indwells me and call that forth**. That will result in life and peace, because God's Spirit has the ability to overcome the lusts of my flesh. Moreover, in this case, it is no longer a war between parts of myself. Now it is a victory orchestrated by the Spirit of Almighty God over my frail frame of dust.

> But if the Spirit of Him who raised Jesus from the dead dwells in you, He who raised Christ from the dead **will also give life to your mortal bodies through His Spirit who dwells in you**. Therefore, brethren, we are debtors — not to the flesh, to live according to the flesh. For if you live according to the flesh you will die; but **if by the Spirit you put to death the deeds of the body, you will live**. For as many as are led by the Spirit of God, these are sons of God (Rom. 8:11-14).

The only way to bring life to our mortal bodies is **through the energizing work of the Holy Spirit. Therefore, I must learn how to energize my body through the Holy Spirit.** I wonder if I have ever heard any sermons on how this is done? I sure hope I have, because this is the very key to New Testament living. Without this, there is no New Testament lifestyle.

To tell you the truth, the church in which I was saved did not know anything about the Holy Spirit. When I finally found a church that preached about life in the Spirit, they simply told me I was to do it. They didn't tell me how. So I had never really been taught how to energize my body through the Holy Spirit who is joined to my spirit. No wonder I was in such a sorry state for so many years. I was missing any understanding of how to apply the central dynamics of New Testament Christianity to my life. No wonder I fell into religion.

How to Energize Your Body Through the Holy Spirit

There is life — power — active energy in the Spirit of God. When one lady touched Jesus for healing, Jesus said that He felt virtue — power — leave Him. *Energis* is one of the three main New Testament words translated "power" and actually means "active energy." There is an active flow of measurable energy that can infiltrate a person's body and flow through it to others, especially when touch is used. Some forms of photography have actually photographed a spark leaving the hand of an evangelist praying for healing for another, and jumping to the other person's body.

> If by the Spirit you put to death the deeds of the body, you shall live...(Rom. 8:13).

There are at least two ways to try to put to death the deeds of the body. One is by the energizing power of the Spirit. The other is by your will power and the strength of your flesh, which really doesn't work. It results in the wretched man syndrome or "will worship," neither of which is life. So we are going to discover how to put to death the deeds of the body by the energy of the Spirit.

Rule One — Become s(S)pirit-conscious.

Learn to sense the energy level of your own spirit by learning how to sense what your spirit feels like. There are probably several ways to do this. I looked up every verse in the Bible on heart and spirit and asked myself, "Have I ever felt the sensation described in this verse within me?" If so, that was a spirit sensation. This process was a great help to me in understanding what the s(S)pirit felt like. An example of what the Bible says you can sense in your spirit would be the ninefold fruit of the Holy Spirit: love, joy, peace...(Gal. 5:22). These are energized emotional states generated by the indwelling presence of the Holy Spirit.

Rule Two — Focus on the Holy Spirit who is joined to your spirit.

I sense Him through vision (the spontaneous picture that alights as I look for God's vision), *rhema* (the spontaneous thoughts that alight as I listen for God's voice), and burden (the spontaneous feelings that are perceived as I wait before God, asking Him to share the emotions of His heart with me). I quiet myself before the Holy Spirit, often using worship or meditating before a Bible story. Or I may sing or pray in the Spirit (Eph. 5:18; Jude 20,21).

Rule Three — Welcome the Holy Spirit's presence.

He is a Person — the third Person of the Trinity. Speak to Him. Welcome Him as a part of your life. Invite His presence to flow within and through you. Tell Him you are open to Him. The Bible teaches that it is possible to grieve the Holy Spirit. I think one of the best ways to do that is to totally ignore Him. I know that when I am ignored, I feel grieved. I also know that when I am recognized and honored, I feel great and want to express myself openly. I believe the same is true of the Holy Spirit. For instance, when through prayer at the beginning of a class I publicly invite the Holy Spirit to flow freely, I find a Spirit of life within that class that is above and beyond the normal class dynamic. I believe it is the Spirit of Life in Christ Jesus we are sensing. This simple act of publicly acknowledging the presence of the Holy Spirit and inviting Him to flow makes all the difference in the world.

Rule Four — Speak forth that which the Holy Spirit is revealing.

Now I will begin to flow with God, speaking out what is bubbling up within me. I am one who is caught up in Divine flow.

> Likewise the Spirit also helps in our weaknesses. For we do not know what we should pray for as we ought, but the Spirit Himself makes intercession for us with groanings which cannot be uttered (Rom. 8:26).

At first I could not believe that God thought I didn't know how to pray. Just listen to me! I can talk to God. However, as we have already seen, anything that "I" do is a dead work, and that includes praying. "I" am not to pray. I am to let God speak through me. That is real prayer. So as I approach God, I quiet myself, look for vision, tune to spontaneity, and begin singing and praying in the Spirit. Gradually I begin to sense a life flow welling up within me. It feels like a pulse of life. It *is* a pulse of life: It is the life of the Holy Spirit energizing my spirit. It feels like power, quickening, peace, love, faith, hope, and joy in the Holy Ghost!

Back to the Law of the Spirit of Life in Christ Jesus

As we said earlier, we believe this is one of the central dynamics to New Testament Christianity. Stated precisely;

The Law of the Spirit of Life in Christ Jesus is the energizing power that one senses within as he fixes his eyes on Jesus, the One who lives within, receiving *rhema*, vision and burden as they fellowship in the Holy Spirit.

This is what sets us free from the law of sin and death. Hallelujah! Now that I know what to do, it is simply a matter of doing it whenever I sense a need for energizing in the Holy Spirit. Therefore, I spend my time worshiping, singing in the Spirit, praying in the Spirit, and tuned to vision and spontaneous flow. I cultivate spontaneous flow by singing freely in the Spirit, making up love songs to the King of kings, while beholding the vision He sets before my eyes. I often enter into the vision John saw in Revelation four of the multitudes worshiping before the throne in heaven. I see the scene as I lift my eyes to look, and I enter into the scene as one of the worshipers. It is so easy from this vantage point to experience energizing Spirit flow within.

In the final analysis, it is really quite child-like. (Wouldn't you have guessed that?) I am a worshiper, living out of my heart rather than my mind. This is something any child can do. Maybe that is why Jesus encouraged us to become like children.

Review of Some Key Points from Chapter Seven

☐ There are two ways to try to keep the Law.

☐ One is to seek to do it yourself.

☐ The other is to do it through the Spirit of Life in Christ Jesus.

☐ The Law of the Spirit of Life in Christ Jesus becomes the central dynamic in New Testament Christianity.

☐ This law ought to be preached regularly.

☐ If this law is not emphasized, we all soon fall back into religion.

☐ This law is defined.

☐ The four rules for energizing our lives through the Holy Spirit are:

Become s(S)pirit-conscious.

Focus on the Holy Spirit who is joined to your spirit.

Welcome the Holy Spirit's presence.

Speak forth that which the Holy Spirit is revealing.

☐ List other points that are important to you.

Think and Discuss

☐ Even though we no longer live by the Law, have you positioned the Law as a safety net under you, so you don't self-destruct if you fall out of the Spirit? Discuss how this works in your life. Give some examples.

- [ ] Are you putting to death the deeds of the flesh through attacking them yourself or through calling upon the power of the Holy Spirit to overcome them?

- [ ] Have you heard other teaching defining and discussing the Law of the Spirit of Life in Christ Jesus? If so, how was it defined? How does it operate? How has it operated in your life in the past? Can you give a detailed example?

- [ ] Write out the author's definition of the Law of the Spirit of Life in Christ Jesus.

- [ ] Discuss together how you have or would apply the four rules for energizing your life through the Holy Spirit.

- [ ] **Journaling** — "Lord, speak to me about the Law of the Spirit of Life in Christ Jesus. How have I been using it? Have I failed to use it?"

- [ ] Second journal entry — "Lord, please talk to me about the rules for energizing my life through your Holy Spirit. What would You like to say concerning the application of these rules to my life?"

Record in your journal what the Lord speaks to you and come prepared to share it in class. As always, it is best if you can actually read a section from your journal.

Chapter Eight

Truth # 7 —
I Live by Faith
That God Is Immanuel

We are near the end now. So far, we have discussed six lessons one must learn in order to overcome the wretched man syndrome and be naturally supernatural, without inner war. We have discovered that God is all and in all, that we are vessels, that we don't live but Christ is our Life, that we are dead to the Law and that it is the Law of the Spirit of Life in Christ Jesus that sets us free from the law of sin and death. That should do it! Armed with this understanding and experience, which comes to me most easily and continuously through journaling, we are ready to live the victorious Christian life. Or are we? Could there be one more roadblock that must be overcome? Yes, I am afraid there is. It is the problem of doubt.

> I have been crucified with Christ; it is no longer I who live, but Christ lives in me; **and the [life] which I now**

**live in the flesh I live by faith in the Son of God, who
loved me and gave Himself for me** (Gal. 2:20).

It is one thing to know all these things academically. It is quite
another to put my faith, hope and trust in them, especially when
I have been so prone to put my faith, hope and trust in my own
abilities and my own reasoning powers. The New Testament
says that "the work of God is to believe...." Is that true! It seems
so often it would be much easier if God's work were something
other than being a believer all the time.

I live in a world (and sometimes a church) that doesn't
believe in fellowship with the Holy Spirit (II Cor. 13:14). Others
think I am crazy because I see visions and hear voices from the
Spirit world on a regular daily basis. Even my mind tells me I
am crazy. "That really isn't God's vision. It is just a figment of
your imagination. That really isn't God's voice. Those are
simply spurious thoughts that are flashing through your mind.
You don't really believe them, do you? You say it is going to
rain, and the entire world is going to drown in a flood? Sure it
is! You are crazy! You say God told you to offer your son on an
altar? Give me a break! You ought to be locked up in a mental
asylum. I have had my fill of religious spooks. Now you say God
told you to march two million people out into the desert and
He is going to care for them supernaturally? Of course He did!
Hey, but get this one: We are going to knock down the walls of
this fortified city today by marching around it and blowing
trumpets! I have had enough! You don't really expect me to
believe such nonsense, do you? I live in the real world. I am not
even sure miracles happen anymore today, much less this kind
of bizarre stuff!"

The truth is that because of your attitude, miracles most
likely don't happen in your world.

And He did not do many mighty works there because
of their unbelief (Matt. 13:58).

Jesus was not able to do many mighty miracles in His hometown because of their unbelief!

The work of God is to believe...

Unbelief is a sin. Unbelief keeps us from the promised land. Unbelief keeps us from enjoying God's provisions. Without faith it is impossible to please Him (Heb. 11:6).

The Example of the Israelites' Struggle with Unbelief

The tragedy of the Old Covenant people is that they would not believe, even when they were watching the supernatural power of God all around them. God said, "Please learn from their mistakes. Please learn to unite faith with My spoken word, so you may enter into My abundance." May we hear the word of the Lord, and may we learn from the stories recorded for us.

Therefore, as the Holy Spirit says: "Today, if you will hear His voice, do not harden your hearts as in the rebellion, in the day of trial in the wilderness, where your fathers tested Me, proved Me, and saw My works forty years. Therefore, I was angry with that generation, and said, 'They always go astray in their heart, and they have not known My ways.' So I swore in My wrath, 'They shall not enter My rest.'" Beware, brethren, lest there be in any of you an evil heart of unbelief in departing from the living God; but exhort one another daily, while it is called 'Today,' lest any of you be hardened through the deceitfulness of sin. For we have become partakers of Christ if we hold the beginning of our confidence steadfast to the end, while it is said: **'Today, if you will hear His voice, do not harden your hearts as in the rebellion.'** For who, having heard, rebelled? Indeed, [was it] not all who came out of Egypt, [led] by Moses? Now with whom was He angry forty years? [Was it] not with those who sinned, whose corpses fell in the wilderness? And to whom did He swear that they would not enter His rest, but to those who **did not obey**? So we see that they could **not enter in because of unbelief**. Therefore, since a promise remains of entering His rest, let us fear lest any of you seem to have come short of it. For indeed the gospel was preached to us as well as to them; but the word which they heard did not profit them, not being mixed with faith in those who heard [it]. For we who have believed do enter that rest, as He has said: "So I swore in My wrath, they shall not enter My rest," although the works were finished from the foundation of the world. (Heb. 3:7-4:3, emphasis added) Again He designates a certain day, saying through David, "Today," after such a long time, as it has been said: **"Today, if you will hear His voice, do not harden your hearts."** For if Joshua had given them rest, then He would not afterward have spoken of another day. There remains therefore a rest for the people of God. For he who has entered His rest has himself also ceased from his works as God [did] from His. **Let us therefore be diligent to enter that rest, lest anyone fall after the same example of disobedience** (Heb. 4:7-11).

What powerful words! "Lord, may we learn to trust You by reading of the examples of Your miraculous working power in ages past. May we not disappoint You and sin against You by not believing in Your goodness and grace and Your voice within our hearts, and trusting instead in the puny workings of our hands and our minds. May we learn to trust You, the true and the living God. Forgive us where we have failed You. Cleanse us, we pray. Let us enter into Your rest. Strengthen our hearts, we pray. Let us believe and do the works that You do, so that the world may behold You in their midst, through us

Your body. Heal us, we pray, and we will be whole. Grant us Thy grace and we will be strong. Grant us Thy faith and we will believe, because it is You who is at work in us to will and to do of Your good pleasure."

A Story

I have been perplexed for some time about the difference I see between the promises of Deuteronomy 28 and the position of the Church of Jesus Christ in the world in which I live. Let's look at the blessings God has promised shall come upon us and overtake us when we act on His words in simple faith.

> Now it shall come to pass, if you diligently obey the voice of the Lord your God, to observe carefully all His commandments which I command you today, that the Lord your God will set you high above all nations of the earth. And all these blessings shall come upon you and overtake you, because you obey the voice of the Lord your God (Deut. 28:1,2).

Wow, not a bad promise! Actually, it is an unbelievable promise to me, because I thought that when I became a Christian I became a second class citizen on this earth. Instead, God promises His covenant people that if they will listen to His voice and obey Him, they will not only be first class, they will become the leading nation upon the earth!

Can we see evidence of this being fulfilled in our day? I think so. Just look at the United States. We put "In God We Trust" on our currency and built our legal system on a Judeo-Christian philosophy. In so doing, we became the most powerful and prosperous nation in the world. There is more to God's promise.

> And the Lord will grant you plenty of goods, in the fruit of your body, in the increase of your livestock, and in the produce of your ground, in the land of which the Lord swore to your fathers to give you. The Lord will

open to you His good treasure, the heavens, to give the rain to your land in its season, and to bless all the work of your hand. You shall lend to many nations, but you shall not borrow. And the Lord will make you the head and not the tail; you shall be above only, and not be beneath, if you heed the commandments of the Lord your God, which I command you today, and are careful to observe [them] (Deut. 28:11-13).

Do you think this describes what the Lord has done for America in the last 200 years? We have lent to many nations (even our enemies), we have not borrowed, at least until recently. In recent years we have turned away from the voice of the Lord our God and some of these promises are waning upon our land as we begin to enter the curse of God as recorded further on in Deuteronomy 28.

I believe these promises are still alive and active for all peoples and all nations of the world today. I believe we can look around the world and see this. However, the thing that bothers me is that in America, Christians are not the head. In many cases, Christians are the borrowers and not the lenders. Polls show a majority of television broadcasters are humanists rather than Christians. I suspect the majority of politicians are humanists, not Christians. I know the majority of television stars are not Christian. The list could go on and on. Why aren't Christians the leaders in America? Do God's promises suddenly no longer work? Is the Bible a lie? No, absolutely not. Then what is the problem? Is the Church of Jesus Christ so far out of touch with the voice of God that we are not able to walk any more in His covenant blessings? Are we no longer listening to His voice and walking in simple obedience to it?

When I was grumbling a year or two ago about the quality of television newscasters, the Lord spoke into my heart and said, "Mark, if you don't like them, why don't you train the next generation of newscasters?" Gulp! I tried to explain to God that I really didn't want to go that far. I just wanted to grumble a little bit. At this point, I was reminded that God slew 14,700 grumblers in the wilderness in one day! And when they grumbled the next day about that, He killed some more. I have really tried to make it a policy in my life not to grumble!

God is not looking for moaners. He is looking for people who will listen to His voice and act on it, and through His power and wisdom and grace bring transformation to the world in which they live.

Will I be one of those people? Will I stop my grumbling long enough to hear what God is saying and in simple child-like faith begin to act in accordance with His *rhema* and vision, in whatever ways He asks me? Will I trust in Him as I go, or will I look to my own ways and abilities to accomplish that which is beyond me? Will I be a believer? Will I train the next generation of newscasters? I don't know. We will have to watch and see. It's enough to scare my flesh to death, which, by the way, isn't a bad thing to have done to your flesh!

Personal Application

Will you be a believer? Will you cast your doubts back to the pit of hell where they came from and believe in the power of Almighty God to intersect your life? Will you be a believer? Will you? You must decide. You must choose either the path of life, faith and hope or the path of fear and dismay. The choice is yours alone. No one else can make it for you. What shall it be? Record your decision in your journal. Write it out so you will have it as a testimony of your place in God. Miracles will follow those who believe. May yours be a miracle-filled life!

Review of Some Key Points from Chapter Eight

☐ God's power and grace are appropriated through faith.

- [ ] The work of God is to believe.
- [ ] The world is prone to doubt.
- [ ] I tend to look at my limitations and to doubt.
- [ ] Religion is prone to believe God no longer moves super-naturally, and to doubt.
- [ ] God wants to supernaturally make us the head and not the tail.
- [ ] God wants us to lead and not follow.
- [ ] God wants us to lend and not borrow.
- [ ] Will the Church rise up in faith and allow God to fill her?
- [ ] Will you?
- [ ] In your journal list other points that were especially impor-tant to you.

Think and Discuss

- [ ] Record some of the unbelievable promises God has given you for your life. What are some of the things He wants to do through you? Are they beyond your abilities? Does that matter? Is God planning to accomplish these promises through your strength and abilities, or His?

- [ ] Are you holding on to the dreams God has placed within your heart? Are you offering them up before God, to see what He wants you to do day by day to fulfill these dreams? Are you doing what He commands? Are you uniting faith to the promises God has given to you? Are you believing He can and will fulfill them if you walk in simple obedience to His voice?

- [ ] Are you a grumbler or a believer? You may want to offer a prayer of repentance for healing and restoration. Repen-tance is the foundation for change. When I grumble, what am I saying about God's ability to rule? How do you think

He feels about that? Do grumblers take into account the supernatural power of God's intervention upon society, or are they simply looking at society and negating God's ability to intervene? How do you think God feels about that? How would you feel about it, if you were God?

☐ God became angry with Moses because he kept explaining to God that because of his poor speech, he could not carry out God's commission for his life. As Moses was complaining, was he taking into account God's supernatural ability to overlay his speaking ability with God's almighty power? Was God expecting Moses to accomplish his mission based on Moses' power or God's power? When God commissions you to do some great feat in this world, is He expecting you to accomplish it through your power or His power? Do you look to yourself to fulfill God's vision for your life, or do you look to God?

☐ Why are Christians not leading in our nation today? Are we supposed to be? What will it take to change this scenario? Will you be a part of the change? Will you become a servant leader in whatever way God is asking you to be? Share your commitment to the vision God has placed within your heart with the other members of the group with which you meet. Then begin journaling about it daily, allowing God to lead you step by step into its fulfillment.

☐ **Journaling** — "Lord, speak to me concerning Your visions for my life. What do You want me to do? What am I supposed to be doing today? What is Your vision for our country? Thank You, Lord, for what You reveal." Come prepared to share with your small group from your journal.

Chapter Nine

Living Naturally Supernatural

Now we have all the parts necessary to overcome the wretched man syndrome and live naturally supernatural, manifesting supernatural life and power and inner peace and rest. We have really come to the conclusion of our book, although I'm not going to stop here. No, I am going to repeat the same truths again and again in the next several chapters so you hear them over and over and over. I am convinced we will not walk in this revelation truth until it has been driven home through much repetition. Years ago, when I first discovered a book with many of these same truths in it, I read the entire book through three times. I knew I wanted to live in that which the book was talking about. It is too precious a truth not to begin to walk in it. A list of other books that speak of this same truth may be found in the Appendix.

The Seven Truths that Allow You to Live Fused to Glory

Truth # 1 — God is all and in all.

Truth # 2 — I am a vessel.

Truth # 3 — I no longer live.

Truth # 4 — Christ is my Life.

Truth # 5 — I am dead to the Law.

Truth # 6 — I live by the Spirit (*rhema* and *vision*).

Truth # 7 — I live by faith that God is Immanuel.

These Seven Truths Applied to Overcoming Temptation

Now let us put these seven truths together and see how they operate when you experience a temptation in your life. It would be nice if there were no more temptations now that we are Christians, but that is not the way it is. Every Christian will testify that we still have them. However, there is a path of victory over them as was exemplified by Jesus, who was tempted in all points as we are, yet was without sin (Heb. 4:15).

How to Let Go and Let God

I had been told many times to "let go and let God," but I never knew how to do that until I discovered the seven truths listed above. Let us take an example. An evil clod comes up and slaps you on the cheek. (He must be an "evil clod" to do such a thing to a wonderful person like you!) Immediately your flesh wants to break his neck, or at least slap him back. However, you remember a command from the Bible that says,

> But I tell you not to resist an evil person. But whoever slaps you on your right cheek, turn the other to him also (Matt. 5:39).

Oh, great, I have to try to love him! So I try. And I try. And I try. But for all my trying, I still want to smack him. I recall the "wretched man syndrome" mentioned in Romans 7:19, where I find myself practicing the very evil I do not wish. I find myself harboring anger toward this individual, no matter how hard I "will" to love him and forgive him.

Then I remember Galatians 3:3.

> Are you so foolish? Having begun in the Spirit, are you now being made perfect by the flesh? (Gal. 3:3)

Of course! I know better than to behave like this! I was saved, not by "my efforts," but by the work of the Holy Spirit. Do I really think I can now perfect myself through "my efforts" rather than the Holy Spirit's? Of course not. "Lord, I am sorry for such foolishness. I repent."

Now I have it:

> No temptation has overtaken you except such as is common to man; but God [is] faithful, who will not allow you to be tempted beyond what you are able, **but with the temptation will also make the way of escape**, that you may be able to beat [it] (I Cor. 10:13).

"Lord, You have provided the way of escape, and I remember what that way is."

> I have been crucified with Christ; it is no longer I who live, but Christ lives in me; and the [life] which I now live in the flesh I live by faith in the Son of God, who loved me and gave Himself for me (Gal. 2:20).

"You have replaced me with Jesus, so now it is the life of Jesus that addresses this situation, not me at all."

> Looking unto Jesus, the author and finisher of [our] faith... (Heb. 12:2).

"Lord Jesus, I come to You. I fix my eyes upon You. Please give me a vision of You handling this situation."

> "My son, remember when My enemies unjustly accused Me, and beat Me and whipped Me and hung Me on a cross

naked and bruised. Remember how I looked down on them from that cross and said to them, 'Father, forgive them, for they know not what they do.' So, too, My son, you have been unjustly accused and humiliated in public, but so, too, My love flows through your heart to forgive your adversaries. See yourself hanging on the cross, repeating My words toward those who have accused you. See My love flowing through your heart as you speak My words. See and you shall be whole. See, My son."

"Yes, my Lord, I see Your love flowing through me to those who have offended me and treated me unjustly, and as I hang there on the cross with You, I speak Your words again: 'Father, forgive them, for they know not what they do.'

"Lord, I feel a change taking place within me. You are breaking the harshness and filling me with Your love. Thank You, my Lord. Thank You for Your wonderful power. I worship You."

There we have it. The entire process all put together. Everything we have said so far in this book has just been dramatized for you in this last story. Did you follow all the parts? They were:

1. I experience a hurt.
2. I see a command telling me how to respond.
3. I try to obey the command and realize I can't.
4. I remember not to try in the flesh but to look to the Spirit.
5. I remember that there is a way of escape through Jesus Christ.
6. I remember that Christ has replaced me and is living through me.
7. I fix my eyes on Jesus and ask Him to respond.
8. He responds with vision, *rhema* and power.
9. I say what He tells me to say and sense His power beginning to flow within my heart.
10. I begin to worship.

Obviously you do not have to try it the wrong way by going first to the Law and self-effort. You can go immediately to the Holy Spirit and say, "Lord, I'm hurt. Would You please speak to me and heal me?" That way you would be skipping steps 2-6 and going immediately from step 1 to step 7. If God's grace allows you to skip the Law and go directly to the Spirit, it is a much more effective way of living.

An Example

Let me say it to you another way: Since Christ is the Light of the world, and sin is usually represented by darkness, we shall let Christ represent light and my temptation represent darkness. *How do you combat darkness?* By pushing it out of the room? Of course not. But that is how many of us try to combat sin in our lives. We kick at it and beat it and try to drive it out. How insane! If you saw me inside a darkened room kicking at the darkness and commanding it to go, you would lock me up. (Not in that room, of course, but in a mental asylum!)

Instead, God wants us to turn the light on. How? By coming to the God who has taken up residence within us and asking Him to reveal Himself to us in the midst of the situation. What are His words? What is His vision of the scene? Jesus said, "The *rhemas* I have spoken to you are Spirit and are life" (John 6:63 NASB and Greek text). With His words and vision comes a flow of Spirit life that sets you free from the law of sin and death, and allows you to live supernaturally fused to Glory.

Another Example

Instead of saying, "Lord, I am trying to love that person. Please help me," you will be saying, "God, I can't love that person, but You can. You are the Source of all love in the universe and You live within me. I ask you to flow out through me and love that person with Your supernatural love." Fix your eyes on the vision of Jesus, as He loved His enemies while hanging on the cross, and as you do, you will begin to sense agape love welling up within you, energizing your inner man and transforming your desires from within. Hallelujah! You will begin to worship as God's love flows out through the pores of your being. Truly Christianity is supernatural after all!

Review of Some Key Points from Chapter Nine

☐ The seven keys to living fused to Glory are:
God is all and in all.
I am a vessel.
I no longer live.
Christ is my life.
I am dead to the Law.
I live by the Spirit (tuned to *rhema* and vision).

☐ I live by faith that God is Immanuel.

☐ Several examples are given of these seven keys in action.

☐ List other points that are important to you.

Think and Discuss

☐ Review a temptation or trial from the past week. How did you handle it? Compare your handling of it to the 10 steps laid out in this chapter. How many of these steps did you go through? Can you identify each step? Have you experienced a trial or temptation recently where you skipped steps two through six and went directly from step one to seven? Share this with your small group. Celebrate the grace of God as manifested in this situation.

☐ Do you try to drive the darkness out of your life, or do you focus on bringing in the Light? Explain specifically what you do. Share the results. What happens?

☐ **Journaling** — "Lord, what do You want to say to me about the way I handle trials and temptations?" Record what He says in your separate journal. Come prepared to share some of it with your small group.

Chapter Ten

Examples of Biblical Characters Learning These Lessons

The Bible is full of stories of people who came to God and had to go through the same process of self-discovery, learning the same lessons we have discussed so far in this book. Often it helps to see someone else walk through the process ahead of you. They become a mentor, showing you where you are going and where to place your feet. Let us examine the stories of four men, two from the Old Testament and two from the New. They are Abraham, Moses, Peter and Paul.

Abraham Learns to Trust God and Not Self (Genesis 12-23)

The story of Abraham opens in Genesis chapter 12, when he is still called Abram.

> Now the Lord had said to Abram: "Get out of your country, from your kindred and from your father's

house, to a land that I will show you. I will make you a great nation; I will bless you and make your name great; and you shall be a blessing. I will bless those who bless you, and I will curse him who curses you; and in you all the families of the earth shall be blessed." So Abram departed as the Lord had spoken to him, and Lot went with him. And Abram [was] seventy-five years old when he departed from Haran (Gen. 12:1-4).

The Lord spoke to Abram and Abram obeyed. That sounds like a follower of God to me. If he were living in New Testament times we would have called him "saved." However, he was living before Christ, so he had an IOU that was paid up at Calvary.

Abram is a follower of God. Has he learned that God is all and in all, and that he is just a vessel that God flows through, or does he still rely on his own abilities to accomplish the work of Almighty God? Let's see.

Now there was a famine in the land, and Abram went down to Egypt to dwell there, for the famine [was] severe in the land. And it came to pass, when he was close to entering Egypt, that he said to Sarai his wife, "Indeed I know that you [are] a woman of beautiful countenance. Therefore it will happen, when the Egyptians see you, that they will say, 'This [is] his wife'; and they will kill me, but they will let you live. Please say you [are] my sister, that it may be well with me for your sake, and that I may live because of you." So it was, when Abram came into Egypt, that the Egyptians saw the woman, that she [was] very beautiful. The princes of Pharaoh also saw her and commended her to Pharaoh. And the woman was taken to Pharaoh's house. He treated Abram well for her sake. He had sheep, oxen, male donkeys, male and female servants, female donkeys, and camels. But the Lord plagued

Pharaoh and his house with great plagues because of Sarai, Abram's wife. And Pharaoh called Abram and said, "What [is] this you have done to me? Why did you not tell me that she [was] your wife? Why did you say, 'She [is] my sister'? I might have taken her as my wife. Now therefore, here is your wife; take [her] and go your way." So Pharaoh commanded [his] men concerning him; and they sent him away, with his wife and all that he had (Gen. 12:10-20).

Abram failed his first test. Even though he was going to be called "the father of faith," he started out by failing miserably in faith, and trusting instead in his cwn reasonings. He was so afraid of God's inability to keep him, he forced his wife to lie and say she was not his wife. That doesn't sound like very great faith to me. As a matter of fact, it sounds a lot like me as I struggle to grow in faith. However, God is not by any means finished. This story is just beginning. So God speaks to Abram again.

Then He brought him outside and said, "Look now toward heaven, and count the stars if you are able to number them." And He said to him, "So shall your descendants be." And he believed in the Lord, and He accounted it to him for righteousness (Gen. 15:5,6).

It appears that Abram is growing in faith in God's Almighty power. God has not only given him a *rhema* word, He has coupled it with vision, and Abram's faith is deepened. Now we should see some results. However, after eleven years of waiting for God to perform His word, Abram began listening to other ways of making it happen. Does that sound like anything you have ever done?

Now Sarai, Abram's wife, had borne him no [children]. And she had an Egyptian maidservant whose name was Hagar. So Sarai said to Abram, "See now, the Lord has restrained me from bearing [children].

Please, go in to my maid; perhaps I shall obtain children by her." And Abram heeded the voice of Sarai (Gen. 16:1,2).

Hagar did conceive and bore a man child, capable of bringing forth a seed line. It looks like man indeed can help God out when things are going slow. We actually have a male child growing up, who could easily be the one through whom the Christ Child will be born. Listen to God's next word to Abram.

When Abram was ninety-nine years old, the Lord appeared to Abram and said to him, "I [am] Almighty God; walk before Me and be blameless" (Gen. 17:1).

In other words, "Walk before Me and quit sinning." Ouch! Was it really that bad, God? I was only trying to help You out. Can't You accept what I have done for You? Listen to Abram's plea.

And Abraham said to God, "Oh, that Ishmael might live before You!" Then God said: "No, Sarah your wife shall bear you a son, and you shall call his name Isaac; I will establish My covenant with him for an everlasting covenant, [and] with his descendants after him" (Gen. 17:18,19).

This is heart-rending. I have tried my best to fulfill the vision God has given to me and I find that He won't accept what I have produced. It is a grand time to backslide and say, "Okay, God, what do You want, anyway? I gave You my best and You don't like it."

You probably know from reading this book what God wants. He doesn't want my best efforts, or my best ideas. He wants me to listen to Him and do only what He instructs me to do. He wants to fill my weakness with His strength and confound the wise by manifesting His wisdom through my ignorance. He doesn't want me to eat from the tree of knowledge of good and evil. He wants me to eat from the tree of life. And I am not to act unless His Spirit is leading me from within. So back to our story.

> And Abraham journeyed from there to the South, and dwelt between Kadesh and Shur, and sojourned in Gerar. Now Abraham said of Sarah his wife, "She [is] my sister." And Abimelech king of Gerar sent and took Sarah. But God came to Abimelech in a dream by night, and said to him, "Indeed you [are] a dead man because of the woman whom you have taken, for she [is] a man's wife" (Gen. 20:1-3).

Seems like we've been through this particular sin before. Abram still cannot trust God to keep him. Instead, he trusts in his own schemes. You see, it takes awhile to become a mighty man of faith and overcome our human weaknesses. It doesn't happen overnight. God places test after test in our lives until we learn to trust Him.

Abraham finally does have a son through Sarah when he is 100 years old. That is 25 years after Abram departed from Haran.

> For Sarah conceived and bore Abraham a son in his old age, at the set time of which God had spoken to him (Gen. 21:2).

> Now Abraham was one hundred years old when his son Isaac was born to him (Gen. 21:5).

The lesson I learn from this is that God often takes longer than I would. I need to beware of impatience. Now, after the promised child has been delivered and the gift of grace is present, we have one final test. Now we will see if Abraham has learned to trust in the power of Almighty God, or if he is still trusting in his own abilities. We will also see if Abraham is going to cling to the gift God has given to him or if he is going to cling to the Lord. Once God has gifted us, it is so easy to cling to that gift rather than to Him.

Now it came to pass after these things that God tested Abraham, and said to him, "Abraham!" And he said, "Here I am." And He said, "Take now your son, your only [son] Isaac, whom you love, and go to the land of Moriah, and offer him there as a burnt offering on one of the mountains of which I shall tell you." So Abraham rose early in the morning and saddled his donkey, and took two of his young men with him, and Isaac his son; and he split the wood for the burnt offering, and arose and went to the place of which God had told him. Then on the third day Abraham lifted his eyes and saw the place afar off. And Abraham said to his young men, "Stay here with the donkey; the lad and I will go yonder and worship, and we will come back to you." So Abraham took the wood of the burnt offering and laid [it] on Isaac his son; and he took the fire in his hand, and a knife, and the two of them went together. But Isaac spoke to Abraham his father and said, "My father!" And he said, "Here I am, my son." And he said, "Look, the fire and the wood, but where [is] the lamb for a burnt offering?" And Abraham said, "My son, God will provide for Himself the lamb for a burnt offering." And the two of them went together. Then they came to the place of which God had told him. And Abraham built an altar there and placed the wood in order; and he bound Isaac his son and laid him on the altar, upon the wood. And Abraham stretched out his hand and took the knife to slay his son. But the Angel of the Lord called to him from heaven and said, "Abraham, Abraham!" And he said, "Here I am." And He said, "Do not lay your hand on the lad, or do anything to him; for now I know that you fear God, seeing you have not withheld your son, your only [son], from Me." Then Abraham lifted his eyes and looked, and there behind [him was] a ram caught in a thicket by its horns. So Abraham went and took the ram, and offered it up for a burnt offering instead of his son. And Abraham called the name of the place, The Lord Will Provide; as it is said [to] this day, "In the Mount of the Lord it shall be provided." Then the Angel of the Lord called to Abraham a second time out of heaven, and said: "By Myself I have sworn, says the Lord, because you have done this thing, and have not withheld your son, your only [son], in blessing I will bless you, and in multiplying I will multiply your descendants as the stars of the heaven and as the sand which [is] on the seashore; and your descendants shall possess the gate of their enemies. In your seed all the nations of the earth shall be blessed, because you have obeyed My voice" (Gen. 22:1-18).

A most hair-raising story! Can you believe Abraham's faith level? What was he thinking as he laid his son on the altar as a sacrifice unto the Lord? Hebrews tells us.

By faith Abraham, when he was tested, offered up Isaac, and he who had received the promises offered up his only begotten [son], of whom it was said, "In Isaac your seed shall be called," **accounting that God [was] able to raise [him] up, even from the dead,** from which he also received him in a figurative sense (Heb. 11:17-19).

Abraham was believing that God was able to raise his son up even from the dead. Now he has become a mighty man of faith, who looks not to his own strength to live life, but to the power of Almighty God. Now, he is a man who lives only out of the voice and vision of Almighty God. May we follow his footsteps!

Moses Learns to Trust God and Not Self (Exodus 1-7)

The story of Moses begins in Exodus 2:10.

> And the child grew, and she brought him to Pharaoh's daughter, and he became her son. So she called his name Moses, saying, "Because I drew him out of the water" (Ex. 2:10).

> By faith [Moses], when he became of age, refused to be called the son of Pharaoh's daughter, choosing rather to suffer affliction with the people of God than to enjoy the passing pleasures of sin, esteeming the reproach of Christ greater riches than the treasures in Egypt; for he looked to the reward (Heb. 11:24-26).

We see that even though Moses grew up in Pharaoh's court, he chose instead to be a follower of Almighty God, even to the point of suffering affliction. It sounds like he was as close as he could be to being a Christian under the Old Covenant. However, even though he had given up all for God, had he learned to trust Almighty God to accomplish all? Let's see.

> Now it came to pass in those days, when Moses was grown, that he went out to his brethren and looked at their burdens. And he saw an Egyptian beating a Hebrew, one of his brethren. So he looked this way and that way, and when he saw no one, he killed the Egyptian and hid him in the sand. And when he went out the second day, behold, two Hebrew men were fighting, and he said to the one who did the wrong, "Why are you striking your companion?" Then he said, "Who made you a prince and a judge over us? Do you intend to kill me as you killed the Egyptian?" So Moses feared and said, "Surely this thing is known!" (Ex. 2:11-14)

Since Moses sensed he was supposed to be a deliverer of his people, he used the only means he knew of to accomplish this purpose: the sword. This was not exactly what God had in mind when He chose Moses to be a deliverer of the captive Jews. God wanted to do the job supernaturally, so the whole world would know that God was in their midst. Do you think God still wants to do that in our generation? Let's follow the story.

> When Pharaoh heard of this matter, he sought to kill Moses. But Moses fled from the face of Pharaoh and dwelt in the land of Midian; and he sat down by a well (Ex. 2:15).

Moses' strength has failed him. His power is broken. He runs and hides in fear. So much for being a deliverer! He is a nothing. He will now go into obscurity in the backside of the wilderness, the place God most often takes those He wants to train for mighty purposes. Is Moses willing to go or does he resist the hand of God and seek a place of prominence? Listen and see.

> Then Moses was **content to live with the man**, and he gave Zipporah his daughter to Moses (Ex.2:21).

When God takes us into obscurity, brokenness and what appears to be failure, we have at least two possible responses. We can kick and scream and protest, or we can go willingly to see what God wants to show us. **Moses went willingly**, and in the desert God showed Him His glory.

> And the Angel of the Lord appeared to him in a flame of fire from the midst of a bush. So he looked, and behold, the bush burned with fire, but the bush [was] not consumed. Then Moses said, "I will now turn aside and see this great sight, why the bush does not burn." So when the Lord saw that he turned aside to look, God called to him from the midst of the bush and said, "Moses, Moses!" And he said, "Here I am." Then He said, "Do not draw near this place. Take your sandals off your feet, for the place where you stand [is] holy

ground." Moreover He said, "I [am] the God of your father — the God of Abraham, the God of Isaac, and the God of Jacob." And Moses hid his face, for he was afraid to look upon God. And the Lord said: "I have surely seen the oppression of My people who [are] in Egypt, and have heard their cry because of their task-masters, for I know their sorrows. So I have come down to deliver them out of the hand of the Egyptians, and to bring them up from that land to a good and large land, to a land flowing with milk and honey, to the place of the Canaanites and the Hittites and the Amorites and the Perizzites and the Hivites and the Jebusites. Now therefore, behold, the cry of the children of Israel has come to Me, and I have also seen the oppression with which the Egyptians oppress them. Come now, therefore, and I will send you to Pharaoh that you may bring My people, the children of Israel, out of Egypt." But Moses said to God, "Who [am] I that I should go to Pharaoh, and that I should bring the children of Israel out of Egypt?" So He said, "I will certainly be with you. And this [shall be] a sign to you that I have sent you: When you have brought the people out of Egypt, you shall serve God on this mountain." Then Moses said to God, "Indeed, [when] I come to the children of Israel and say to them, 'The God of your fathers has sent me to you,' and they say to me, 'What [is] His name?' what shall I say to them?" And God said to Moses, "I AM WHO I AM." And He said, "Thus you shall say to the children of Israel, 'I AM has sent me to you.' " Moreover God said to Moses, "Thus you shall say to the children of Israel: 'The Lord God of your fathers, the God of Abraham, the God of Isaac, and the God of Jacob, has sent me to you. This [is] My name forever, and this [is] My memorial to all generations.' Go and gather the elders of Israel together, and say to them, 'The Lord God of your fathers, the God of Abraham, of Isaac, and of Jacob, appeared to me, saying, "I have surely visited you and [seen] what is done to you in Egypt; and I have said I will bring you up out of the affliction of Egypt to the land of the Canaanites and the Hittites and the Amorites and the Perizzites and the Hivites and the Jebusites, to a land flowing with milk and honey." ' Then they will heed your voice; and you shall come, you and the elders of Israel, to the king of Egypt; and you shall say to him, "The Lord God of the Hebrews has met with us; and now, please, let us go three days' journey into the wilderness, that we may sacrifice to the Lord our God." But I am sure that the king of Egypt will not let you go, no, not even by a mighty hand. So I will stretch out My hand and strike Egypt with all My wonders which I will do in its midst; and after that he will let you go. And I will give this people favor in the sight of the Egyptians; and it shall be, when you go, that you shall not go empty handed. But every woman shall ask of her neighbor, namely, of her who dwells near her house, articles of silver, articles of gold, and clothing; and you shall put [them] on your sons and on your daughters. So you shall plunder the Egyptians." Then Moses answered and said, "But suppose they will not believe me or listen to my voice; suppose they say, 'The Lord has not appeared to you.' " So the Lord said to him, "What [is] that in your hand?" And he said, "A rod." And He said, "Cast it on the ground." So he cast it on the ground, and it became a serpent; and Moses fled from it. Then the Lord said to Moses,

"Reach out your hand and take [it] by the tail" (and he reached out his hand and caught it, and it became a rod in his hand), "that they may believe that the Lord God of their fathers, the God of Abraham, the God of Isaac, and the God of Jacob, has appeared to you." Furthermore the Lord said to him, "Now put your hand in your bosom." And he put his hand in his bosom, and when he took it out, behold, his hand [was] leprous, like snow. And He said, "Put your hand in your bosom again." So he put his hand in his bosom again, and drew it out of his bosom, and behold, it was restored like his [other] flesh. "Then it will be, if they do not believe you, nor heed the message of the first sign, that they may believe the message of the latter sign. And it shall be, if they do not believe even these two signs, or listen to your voice, that you shall take water from the river and pour [it] on the dry [land]. And the water which you take from the river will become blood on the dry [land]." Then Moses said to the Lord, "O my Lord, I [am] not eloquent, neither before nor since You have spoken to Your servant; but I [am] slow of speech and slow of tongue." So the Lord said to him, "Who has made man's mouth? Or who makes the mute, the deaf, the seeing, or the blind? [Have] not I, the Lord? Now therefore, go, and I will be with your mouth and teach you what you shall say." But he said, "O my Lord, please send by the hand of whomever [else] You may send." So the anger of the Lord was kindled against Moses, and He said: "Is not Aaron the Levite your brother? I know that he can speak well. And look, he is also coming out to meet you. When he sees you, he will be glad in his heart. Now you shall speak to him and put the words in his mouth. And I will be with your mouth and with his mouth, and I will teach you what you shall do. So he shall be your spokesman to the people. And he himself shall be as a mouth for you, and you shall be to him as God. And you shall take this rod in your hand, with which you shall do the signs" (Ex. 3:2- 4:17).

What a drama! Alone in the desert — that is where we most often discover the power of God. Moses received his revelation of God there, as did Paul, and even Jesus began His supernatural ministry after 40 days alone in the desert. Will you willingly follow God to the desert if He leads you there?

Notice Moses' reluctance to be mightily used by God. Moses is still looking at his limitations: his inability to speak fluently, his lack of credibility. God became downright angry with him, because he would not accept the fact that **God was going to speak through him and be his mouthpiece.** God does not want us to look at our limitations. If we are living out of His Spirit and His power and His wisdom, we have no limitations other than those of Almighty God, and there are none! God wants to raise up a generation of men and women who will listen only to the voice and vision of Almighty God, and do only what He commands them; through them God will transform this world. All He needs is a people. Will you be part of this band of people who learn to hear the voice of God and see His vision, leaning not on your own understanding but in all your ways acknowledging Him? If so, God will use you to mightily change this world. He does not need wise or powerful people. He needs people who live only out of Divine initiative as Jesus did. These are the people who transform the world in which they live.

Now look what God does for Moses.

So the Lord said to Moses: "See, I have made you [as] God to Pharaoh, and Aaron your brother shall be your prophet" (Ex. 7:1).

The word "as" is not in the original Hebrew text. Therefore, it actually reads, "...See, I have made you God to Pharaoh..." When we release the supernatural power of God through our lives, we appear as God to the world in which we live. The New Testament phrase is that we are "the body of Christ." Moses now is a supernatural deliverer, no longer trusting in the strength of his right hand to overcome the enemy, but trusting in the flow of the supernatural power of God out through his life to bring millions into freedom from captivity.

We will either appear as God to those around us, because we are releasing the Divine power of Almighty God through our lives, or we will become the laughingstock of the world as we enter into religious systems. The choice is ours.

Peter Learns to Trust God and Not Self

Now we turn to the New Testament, and we look first at Peter, a man who had left all to follow Jesus.

> Then Peter began to say to Him, "See, we have left all and followed You" (Mark 10:28).

Again, that sounds about as saved as you could be before the death and resurrection of Jesus Christ. However, had Peter learned to trust the power of Almighty God, or was he still trusting in his own power to establish the Kingdom? The story of the breaking of Peter's self-sufficiency is recorded in Luke 22:31-61. We will read parts of it.

> And the Lord said, "Simon, Simon! Indeed, satan has asked for you, that he may sift [you] as wheat. But I have prayed for you, that your faith should not fail; and when you have returned to [Me], strengthen your brethren." But he said to Him, "Lord, I am ready to go with You, both to prison and to death." Then He said, "I tell you, Peter, the rooster will not crow this day

> before you will deny three times that you know Me"
> (Luke 22:31-34).
>
> Peter answered and said to Him, "Even if all are
> made to stumble because of You, I will never be
> made to stumble" (Matt. 26:33).

Here we see that Peter is cocky and self-confident, trusting in his own strength to keep him. "I will never...." We see that sufficient "I" lurking yet in Peter's life, even though he is a follower of Jesus, and has left all to follow Him. Now God is going to take Peter through the breaking process. When Judas betrayed Jesus,

> Simon Peter, having a sword, drew it and struck the
> high priest's servant, and cut off his right ear. The
> servant's name was Malchus. Then Jesus said to Peter,
> "Put your sword into the sheath. Shall I not drink the
> cup which My Father has given Me?" (John 18:10,11)

That is enough to throw any devout believer into confusion. Here I am defending God with all my might, and He is actually working against me and on the side of those who want to destroy Him! Worse than that, Jesus thinks it is God's will that His life be unjudiciously destroyed. This absolutely does not make any sense.

Life doesn't make any sense if you are not tuned to the Divine initiative, because God's ways are not our ways and God's thoughts are not our thoughts. It is like an upside down kingdom, where the first are last and the last are first, and if you save your life you lose it and if you lose your life you save it. I could never figure out the plans and purposes of God. The nice thing is, I don't have to. God reveals them through His prophets. And in the Church we have all become prophets, priests and kings unto the Most High God. So we can ask God what is going on and most often He tells us.

Before the night is over, Peter has denied Jesus three times and gone out and wept bitterly. Before many days are past, he has totally given up and gone back to fishing. **Now** he is fit for the Master's use. Now he has come to the end of himself. Now he sees that he can do nothing through his might or his wisdom to build the kingdom of God. The tree of knowledge has proven to be of no avail. Now as a broken man, he is fit for use.

Jesus heals Peter in John 21 and recommissions him into the ministry: "Feed my sheep." Then Peter waits for power from on high before he moves again.

> Now when the Day of Pentecost had fully come, they were all with one accord in one place. And suddenly there came a sound from heaven, as of a rushing mighty wind, and it filled the whole house where they were sitting. Then there appeared to them divided tongues, as of fire, and [one] sat upon each of them. And they were all filled with the Holy Spirit and began to speak with other tongues, as the Spirit gave them utterance (Acts 2:1-4).

Peter is now prepared to enter into supernatural ministry. Notice his daily activity.

> Now Peter and John went up together to the temple at the hour of prayer, the ninth [hour] (Acts 3:1).

He has learned to begin his day with prayer, seeking the Divine initiative and the Divine flow of power so that he builds with supernatural power and wisdom. God had completed the lesson. He had taken Peter through drastic self-exposure, which left him broken and discouraged. God then healed Peter's heart, recommissioned him, anointed him with power and sent him forth. That is exactly the same process He utilizes with each of us. Where are you in the process?

Paul Learns to Trust God and Not Self

Finally, we come to Paul, the last person in our current study. Let us see how God taught Paul to trust in the supernatural power of Almighty God rather than the limited resources of man.

Paul describes his childhood training and commitment to God in Philippians three.

> Though I also might have confidence in the flesh. If anyone else thinks he may have confidence in the flesh, I more so: circumcised the eighth day, of the stock of Israel, [of] the tribe of Benjamin, a Hebrew of the Hebrews; concerning the law, a Pharisee; concerning zeal, persecuting the church; concerning the right-eousness which is in the law, blameless (Phil. 3:4-6).

If anyone was committed to Almighty God, Paul was. He had the best religious upbringing possible, he was fervent, he kept the Law perfectly and lived what he believed by persecuting those whom he considered heretics. He studied the Law of God with great earnestness and devotion, and applied it meticulously to his life. However, for all Paul had going for him, he was still operating out of human reasoning and understanding, and human power and might. He was living out of the tree of knowledge of good and evil. He was not one who walked in Divine encounter. He was not one who heard the voice of God or saw the vision of God. He was one who lived out of biblical law. He was very much like I was during the first ten years of my Christian life. I, too, lived out of Biblical law. I could not hear the Lord's voice or see vision. I operated out of human strength and human wisdom. I accused others in the Church with whom I did not agree. I was a model Pharisee. Ouch!

Then God said, "This has gone far enough. I see Paul's heart. He is actually seeking Me, even though he is coming against My Church. He is just a bit confused and misled. I am going to meet with him and straighten him out." And did they meet! It was on the Damascus Road:

Then Saul, still breathing threats and murder against the disciples of the Lord, went to the high priest and asked letters from him to the synagogues of Damascus, so that if he found any who were of the Way, whether men or women, he might bring them bound to Jerusalem. And as he journeyed he came near Damascus, and suddenly a light shone around him from heaven. Then he fell to the ground, and heard a voice saying to him, "Saul, Saul, why are you persecuting Me?" And he said, "Who are You, Lord?" And the Lord said, "I am Jesus, whom you are persecuting. [It is] hard for you to kick against the goads." So he, trembling and astonished, said, "Lord, what do You want me to do?" And the Lord [said] to him, "Arise and go into the city, and you will be told what you must do." And the men who journeyed with him stood speechless, hearing a voice but seeing no one. Then Saul arose from the ground, and when his eyes were opened he saw no one. But they led him by the hand and brought [him] into Damascus. And he was three days without sight, and neither ate nor drank. Now there was a certain disciple at Damascus named Ananias; and to him the Lord said in a vision, "Ananias." And he said, "Here I am, Lord." So the Lord [said] to him, "Arise and go to the street called Straight, and inquire at the house of Judas for [one] called Saul of Tarsus, for behold, he is praying. And in a vision he has seen a man named Ananias coming in and putting [his] hand on him, so that he might receive his sight." Then Ananias answered, "Lord, I have heard from many about this man, how much harm he has done to Your saints in Jerusalem. And here he has authority from the chief priests to bind all who call on Your name." But the Lord said to him, "Go, for he is a chosen vessel of Mine to bear My name before Gentiles, kings, and the children of Israel. For I will show him how many things he must suffer for My name's sake." And Ananias went his way and entered the house; and laying his hands on him he said, "Brother Saul, the Lord Jesus, who appeared to you on the road as you came, has sent me that you may receive your sight and be filled with the Holy Spirit." Immediately there fell from his eyes [something] like scales, and he received his sight at once; and he arose and was baptized. And when he had received food, he was strengthened. Then Saul spent some days with the disciples at Damascus. Immediately he preached the Christ in the synagogues, that He is the Son of God (Acts 9:1-20).

Wow! What an incredible story! We just moved from religion to supernatural Christianity! We just moved from the tree of knowledge to the tree of life, from human power to Divine power, from living out of our own abilities to living out of Divine encounter. This change must be made in each Christian's life. It must be made in my life. It must be made in yours. Has it been made in your life yet?

I said earlier that confusion is often the first step to revelation. Well, Paul obviously went through some confusion when he realized that everything he had believed and stood for and done was wrong, and he now had to go back and restudy and re-experience everything he had been taught. So Paul got away from everyone except God.

Nor did I go up to Jerusalem to those [who were] apostles before me; but I went to Arabia, and returned again to Damascus. Then after three years... (Gal. 1:17,18).

Each of us must be willing to get alone and discover God within our own spirits. He is more than a theology, which I can learn from another. He is an actual Person who wants to live and move within me and around me and through me. And the only way to discover Him is to actually take some time to learn to sense His movements within and through me. This is experience-oriented learning. This is not textbook learning. This is learning by feeling. I feel the presence and power of God. I see His vision. I hear His voice. This is not discovered in a textbook. This is discovered as I plunge into the depths of my heart.

After three years, Paul re-entered society. First he went down to Jerusalem to submit his new understandings and experiences with God to the established church leaders there. Once he was able to have his new experiences and interpretations covered by those in spiritual authority, he began preaching them powerfully.

> Then after three years I went up to Jerusalem to see Peter, and remained with him fifteen days. But I saw none of the other apostles except James, the Lord's brother. (Now [concerning] the things which I write to you, indeed, before God, I do not lie.) Afterward I went into the regions of Syria and Cilicia; and I was unknown by face to the churches of Judea which [were] in Christ. But they were hearing only, "He who formerly persecuted us now preaches the faith which he once [tried to] destroy." And they glorified God in me (Gal. 1:18-24).

With His new theology covered, Paul begins ministering again. But his new ministry is supernatural. He heals the sick and raises the dead. He is now a vessel that releases the supernatural power of almighty God.

> But what things were gain to me, these I have counted loss for Christ. But indeed I also count all things loss for the excellence of the knowledge of Christ Jesus my Lord, [Greek, ginosko, "intimate experiencing of"] for whom I have suffered the loss of all things, and count

them as rubbish, that I may gain Christ and be found in Him, [Paul's new life is found by living in a Person — the Person of Christ] not having my own righteousness, which [is] from the law, but that which [is] through faith in Christ, **the righteousness which is from God by faith**; that I may know [*ginosko*] Him **and the power of His resurrection, and the fellowship of His sufferings, being conformed to His death, if, by any means, I may attain to the resurrection from the dead** (Phil. 3:7-11).

Paul has gone through a personal death and resurrection. He sees that it is no longer he who lives, but now it is Christ who lives His life out through him. Hallelujah! Paul now lives sensitized to the flow of the Holy Spirit's power within him. He no longer lives out of his mind. He now lives out of his heart, and the tree of life within his heart. He is living fused to glory!

Two Key Turning Points in the Christian's Life

There are two key turning points in the Christian's life. One is salvation, when you find Christ (actually, He finds you). The other is when Galatians 2:20 is fully experienced in your life. Have you experienced both? If not, go to the desert and discover Him, the One who flows effortlessly within your being.

After our salvation experience, a period of struggle and failure generally occurs. Finally, we realize we have died with Christ and that we have risen with Him. It is as if I have $50,000 in the bank, but in my ignorance I believe it is only $5,000. I try to live on the $5,000 level until I finally discover my mistake and cash a second check — the second blessing, as some have called it.

Review of Some Key Points from Chapter Ten

☐ The Bible records many stories of men and women who learned to trust God and not self.

☐ This is a lesson we all must learn.

☐ In learning this lesson, we move from religion to supernatural Christianity.

☐ We often discover the power of God in the desert.

☐ We must be willing to go to the desert to discover the flow of God.

☐ Once self is broken, we can live fused to glory. Supernatural power begins flowing through us.

☐ List other points which are especially important to you.

Think and Discuss

☐ Do you agree that confusion often precipitates revelation? Have you ever gone through a time of confusion which gave birth to greater revelation? Is so, recall that experience. In light of this, do you think it might be wise to celebrate our times of confusion, knowing that God is disorienting us so He can give us a new orientation?

☐ Have you gone through steps similar to those followed by the four biblical characters studied in this chapter? If so, recall the stages of your life, as they relate to the theme of this chapter. Where are you now? What stage are you in? What is the next step God is asking you to take? Are you preparing yourself to take it? Are you flowing with the purposes and power of God or are you resisting for all you are worth? As Moses, are you **willingly** submitting to the purposes of God in your life?

☐ **Journaling** — "Lord, please speak to me concerning the stages of my Christian walk. Where am I? Where are You taking me? How do You want me to respond right now?" Record journal what the Lord says, and come prepared to share it with your small group.

Chapter Eleven

The Skills Acquired in the Wilderness

It is interesting to notice how often God takes those He is preparing into the wilderness for a period of time as part of their training. Why do you suppose He does that? Is there something in the wilderness that we cannot find in society? If so, what? Does God take us there to make us miserable? To destroy all our hopes and ambitions? Why does He take us to the wilderness?

Has God taken you to the wilderness? If so, when? What did you learn there? Did He accomplish within your heart and soul what He wanted to accomplish? We need to explore the answers to these and many other questions, so we can learn to pass quickly through our wilderness experiences and move on into the promised land.

God Is the One Who Leads Us into the Wilderness

Remember that when God led the Israelites, He led them into the wilderness. The same was true of Jesus:

Then Jesus, being filled with the Holy Spirit, returned from the Jordan and was led by the Spirit into the wilderness (Luke 4:1).

I don't just wander into the wilderness. God chooses the times that are right for me and leads me into the wilderness. He has some special purposes in mind. He knows this is what I need. In the flesh, it is so hard for me to see this. I have been enjoying myself in society. I may have a stable life, with food, clothing and all my needs met. To go to a place where I can no longer count on any of these things being provided by my hand is scary.

The Wilderness Is Where Self-Reliance Is Broken

I immediately come face to face with the fact that I cannot provide for myself very adequately in the wilderness. This may be a literal wilderness or God may have simply taken me out of an established job, and brought me into a transitional period where I am forced to trust in Him. In any case, it is a place where self-reliance is broken. It is a place where I am to learn not to trust in the strength of my right arm but rather in the power of Almighty God to be my Provider and Sustainer. God provided food supernaturally to the Israelites day by day as they walked in the wilderness. It was there that they learned that weakness yielded to strength is the lifestyle of God's children.

I have walked through several transition times and wilderness experiences, and as I journal God continuously tells me that He is my Provider and Sustainer, and that I am to trust in Him. He says it over and over. Following is just one example:

11-26-89

"Good morning, Jesus. I sense You want to restore me this day. I sense You have already begun the restoration process during the night."

"Yes, My son, I have. I have begun it during the night. I have had angels ministering to you. And now this day I shall again have angels ministering to you. You are My beloved son in whom I am well pleased."

"But, Lord, I fail You so much."

"Mark, I am giving you tests you have never had before. I am stretching you for the work whereunto I have called you. That is why you feel a sense of failure, because you are struggling to expand your faith as I told you to do earlier this year."

"Yes, Lord, I do remember that You commissioned me to expand my faith. I guess I almost forgot that."

"And, son, the rest of your explorations are simply that — explorations. That is okay. That is the way I have built man. Do not be dismayed, for I am with you.

"Mark, expand your faith, for I am going to do wonderful things through your life. I shall not leave you nor forsake you. I will be with you. Relax and trust in Me. Continue to write and experiment and lecture...you are so important to Me. That is why I am pruning you and strengthening you, for I have great things in store for you. Great things we shall build together. However, you must be purified and strengthened. Therefore, My son, celebrate the process, because the process is that which you are in. You cannot celebrate the end goal this day because you cannot even bear to look upon the end goal. Therefore, celebrate the process. And again I say, celebrate the process.

"I will send others to strengthen you at this time. That is how My body works. You strengthen others when you see the goal, they strengthen you when they see the goal. Receive those I send to you."

"Yes, my Lord."

"My son, you shall again go onto the highways and byways and tell the Word. However, at this time I have called you home to prepare the vessel and the word I shall have him to speak. Pray for the full release of all things and I shall speed them on their way. In the meantime, I have and I shall continue to meet your every need. Watch and see."

The Lord then gave me instructions on how to love my wife more completely and the next action He wanted me to take that day.

You see, God is stretching me. He is teaching me to trust in Him and understand the place He has me right now in my life and the purpose for being there, as well as how I am to respond while I am there. Such wisdom and strength flow into my life when I journal. And it is not simply esoteric wisdom. He ended with practical advice on daily living.

The Wilderness Is Where We Learn to Quit Grumbling

Numbers 11 through 18 record several times that the people and Moses grumbled against God. Generally this brought forth God's anger and a severe consequence. You may want to read these chapters to see some of the stories detailing the things God was dealing with in the hearts of His people. He was cleaning out pride, envy, greed, jealousy, unbelief, and lack of thankfulness for all things. On one day, God killed 14,700 people who were grumbling (Num. 17:49). When I noticed that, I decided to give up grumbling for Lent (actually for life). God hates grumbling. He has commanded us to rejoice evermore, and in everything give thinks, because He is Lord over all. When we grumble, we fail to acknowledge His lordship over all, and enter into self-centeredness and unbelief.

Just to set the record straight, I still do have my times of grumbling. They occur every time I fall out of the presence of God and go back into self-consciousness. Therefore, grumbling has become a barometer of the presence of God in my life. Even Moses became depressed from time to time.

> If You treat me like this, please kill me here and now
> — if I have found favor in Your sight — and do not
> let me see my wretchedness! (Num. 11:15)

I can identify with that. "God, please take me so I don't have to see how wretched I become when I fall out of Your presence." It is such a reminder of who I am. It certainly is a good thing I am learning to live fused to Glory.

Obviously, many of the negative thoughts that go through our minds during periods of testing are being sent by the devil. When Jesus was in the wilderness (Luke 4), He had a conversation with the devil. Satan tempted Him to use His strength to provide for Himself: "Tell this stone to become bread." Satan was accusative in his tone: "If You are the Son of God..." Satan appealed to His pride and ego: "I will give You all this dominion and its glory..." Satan tempted Jesus to test God, but Jesus answered, "You shall not put the Lord your God to the test." Satan even used Scriptures in his attack; that is, Scriptures out of context.

Therefore, part of what is happening in our wilderness experience is that we are coming face to face with the satanic, negative, accusative, prideful, greedy thoughts within our hearts and minds, recognizing they are the voice of satan, and overcoming them by replacing them with the voice of Almighty God. The wilderness is a place and time in our lives where we discover and remove the demonic voice within us, and recognize and flow with the Divine voice within us.

The Wilderness Is Where We Learn to Hear God's Voice

In Deuteronomy 5:22-31, Moses is recounting the story of God's attempt to restore His voice and fellowship to His covenant children. He had created mankind so that He could have fellowship with us. And He did commune with Adam and Eve for a time, until sin broke that fellowship. Now, in the wilderness, God is seeking to restore fellowship with His children by offering to the Israelites His voice. However, with His voice comes fire, which we know to be the purifying work of the Holy Spirit in our lives as He burns off the sin, bringing us through a death in our flesh so we can fully live from our spirits. The Israelites were not so sure they wanted to go through this death process. It might hurt. So they turned down God's voice and chose instead to live under biblical Law. There is a place for biblical Law, as we have already discussed. It keeps me in custody until I learn to hear God's voice, and it teaches me that my flesh does not have the power to perfect me.

So the Israelites rejected God's voice. That is why they never arrived at the Promised Land, but all died in the wilderness. The promised land is the fruit of living out of the voice and vision of Almighty God. Even as their children conquered the cities that were in the promised land, they did so through obeying the Divine directives that were given to them from the voice of God.

The desert is the place we are supposed to learn to hear God's voice and come into obedience to it. If you miss this lesson, you may never come out of the desert in your life. If you have not yet learned to hear God's voice, I recommend you read my testimony in Dialogue With God. If you know how to hear God's voice and simply are not listening and obedient on a regular basis, please repent and make a new start, so you can get on with your life.

Key Points from Chapter Eleven

The wilderness is an important part of each of our lives.

☐ There are key lessons we are to learn in the wilderness.

☐ God leads us into the wilderness when the time is right.

☐ If we learn the lessons God has designed for us, God leads us out of the wilderness.

☐ If we do not learn the lessons God has designed for us, we may never come out of the wilderness, but may instead die there.

☐ On the other side of the wilderness is the Promised Land.

☐ List other points that were significant to you.

Think and Discuss

☐ Have you been to the wilderness yet? Did you learn the lessons God was trying to teach you there? What were they? How has your life changed as a result of obedience to these lessons? Share these with your small group.

☐ Have you discovered the voice of God within your heart? Have you discovered the voice of the accuser within your heart? Have you cast down the accuser, and embraced the Comforter within? Are you listening and obedient to the voice of God?

☐ Have you gone willingly when God has led you into the wilderness? Have you submitted to His hand so that He can teach you and bring you forth fused to Glory? Share your experiences with your small group.

☐ **Journaling** — "Lord, what do You want to say to me concerning my wilderness experience? Where was it? What was it? What were You trying to teach me? Have I learned? Am I willingly flowing with You, or am I resisting You as You take me by the hand? Thank You, Lord, for what You speak." As always, write these questions in a separate journal, quieting yourself in the presence of the Lord and tuning to spontaneity. Record what He says to you. Come prepared to share from your journal with those in your small group.

Chapter Twelve

Rereading the New Testament

In light of my discovery of the seven truths in the earlier part of this book, I reread the New Testament and found it to be an entirely new Book. It came alive like never before, and burned with deeper revelation in my heart than I had ever experienced. Let's go through a few parts of it together and see what we can find. Before we do, let us recall together the seven key truths of this book.

Truth # 1 — God is all and in all.

Truth # 2 — I am a vessel.

Truth # 3 — I no longer live.

Truth # 4 — Christ is my Life.

Truth # 5 — I am dead to the Law.

Truth # 6 — I live by the Spirit (tuned to rhema and vision).

Truth # 7 — I live by faith that God is Immanuel.

Traveling through Romans Six, Seven and Eight

Romans six, seven and eight offer three fascinating stages of the Christian's life. Romans six corresponds to our salvation experience. Romans seven deals with the struggle we face before we learn to live "in Christ," and Romans eight describes the life of peace and power we experience after we have learned that we have died and our life is hidden with God in Christ. You may want to prayerfully read these chapters now before going on.

Paul talks of our salvation experience in Romans 6:4.

> Therefore we were buried with Him through baptism into death, that just as Christ was raised from the dead by the glory of the Father, even so we also should walk in newness of life (Rom. 6:4).

Now that I have gone through the waters of baptism, I am ready to begin my Christian life. I know that my old self was crucified with Him (6:6). I consider myself dead to sin and alive to God in Christ Jesus (6:11), and I act accordingly, no longer letting sin reign in my mortal body. Sounds simple enough, doesn't it? Know it, consider it and act it. There, that should do it. I am on my merry way except...what is this battle I am feeling?

> For the good that I will [to do], I do not do; but the evil I will not [to do], that I practice....I find then a law, that evil is present with me, the one who wills to do good. For I delight in the law of God according to the inward man. But I see another law in my members, warring against the law of my mind, and bringing me into captivity to the law of sin which is in my members. O wretched man that I am! Who will deliver me from this body of death? (Rom. 7:19,21-24)

There must be more to it than knowing, considering and acting. I am in a war! I am in the wretched man syndrome. Help! Yes, there is more.

> For the law of the Spirit of life in Christ Jesus has made
> me free from the law of sin and death (Rom. 8:2).

Aha! So there is another law I was forgetting about (or hadn't learned about yet). It is the Law of the Spirit of Life in Christ Jesus. That sounds exciting. Now I am getting beyond thinking, considering and acting. Now I am down to the spirit level, and I am not just touching my spirit. I am touching the Spirit of Christ who is joined to my spirit, and sensing His life flow. I am focusing myself on the flow of Spirit power within my spirit (8:5,6) and sensing an energizing flow throughout my whole body (8:11). I feel a tremendous intimacy with God as I sense His movements within my heart (8:15,16). Now He leads me from within my heart. I even feel deep sensations within my spirit that direct me as I pray (8:26). I do nothing out of my own thoughts or power. I always look within and discover His power and pulse of life, and I live out of that pulse. Glory be to God! He has set me free from my own self. He has made me "God-conscious" rather than "self-conscious."

Rereading Colossians

Formerly, when I went to Paul's books, I would head straight for the second half because that was the practical, down-to-earth part that told me how to live and behave and act. That was the "meat" of the book, I thought. Besides, the first half was full of a lot of mumble jumble about being in Christ, which I really didn't understand very well.

Now I see that by skipping over the first half of these books and rushing directly into the second half, I was missing the foundational truths which empower me to do the actions called for in the second half. I am not expected to do them at all, but Christ does them in and through me. For example, let's look at the letter to the Colossians. You may want to read the first three chapters before going on.

The following is a record of my meditations on Colossians chapters one through three. Watch for the subtle shifts in the conversation as the truths of the passage become more and more personal.

First, we find Paul reiterating what he considers to be the "abiding realities" of life: faith, hope and love (Col. 1:4,5; cf. I Cor. 13:13). I acknowledge these as a barometer of how thoroughly I am living in Christ. When I am saturated with His presence, I am full of faith, hope and love. When I am distant from His presence, these three realities are no longer evident through me. Now let's jump down to verse 10:

> ...that you may have a walk worthy of the Lord, fully pleasing [Him], being fruitful in every good work and increasing in the knowledge of God (Col. 1:10).

"There, that's more like it!" I used to say. "Now I have a command I can try to obey. I can try to walk worthy of the Lord. Let's go for it!" I didn't realize in years past that the margin of my Bible (NASB) put the words "real knowledge" as the literal meaning of the word "knowledge" in the above. What? Is there both "knowledge" and "true knowledge?" Could it be something like head knowledge and heart knowledge, or the tree of knowledge and the tree of life? Oh, well, no time to worry about that, I have a command I am supposed to obey! "I" am supposed to walk in a manner worthy of the Lord. Now, let's go on to the next verses.

> ...strengthened with all might, **according to His glorious power,** for all patience and long-suffering with joy; giving thanks **to the Father who has qualified us** to be partakers of the inheritance of the saints in the light (Col. 1:11,12).

Interesting! Maybe it is God's glorious power that strengthens me to walk in a manner worthy. Maybe it is He who qualifies me.

> He has delivered us from the power of darkness and translated [us] into the kingdom of the Son of His love (Col. 1:13).

I never noticed that! It all centers around the work of God rather than around me.

> ...in whom we have redemption through His blood, the forgiveness of sins (Col. 1:14).

Again, my redemption is not through my efforts. It is through God's efforts.

> For it pleased [the Father that] in Him all the fullness should dwell (Col. 1:19).

God has put the entire fulness of the Deity in His Son Jesus. Jesus manifests all the power of the entire universe.

> ...In the body of His flesh through death, to present you holy, and blameless, and irreproachable in His sight (Col. 1:22).

Because of the work of Christ, I am presented irreproachable in God's sight. You mean it is not what I do that makes me irreproachable? My beauty is based on what Christ has done? Interesting! Maybe I should lighten up and just relax a bit more into the finished work of Jesus.

> ...if indeed you continue in the faith, grounded and steadfast, and are not moved away from the hope of the gospel which you heard, which was preached to every creature under heaven, of which I, Paul, became a minister (Col. 1:23).

I knew there had to be an "if clause" in here somewhere. This was just too good to be true. I am irreproachable if I walk in righteousness, right? No, you are irreproachable if you believe in the finished work of Christ within your heart. Believe? That's it? Just believe? Believe what?

The mystery which has been hidden from ages and from generations, but now has been revealed to His saints. To them God willed to make known what are the riches of the glory of this mystery among the Gentiles: which is Christ in you, the hope of glory (Col. 1:26,27).

I must believe in the great mystery. What is that great mystery? It is that **Christ lives in you,** and He is your only hope of ever becoming glorious. Rather than believing in my own strength to make me glorious, I am supposed to believe in His strength within me to make me glorious.

Him we preach, warning every man and teaching every man in all wisdom, that we may **present every man perfect in Christ Jesus** (Col. 1:28).

So it is **Him** you are preaching. I formerly **preached about me,** and my striving to be holy, and my efforts, and my guilt, and my failings, and my.... I always used to preach about self and what self should do, but self doesn't live anymore. Let's preach instead about Someone who does live within the heart of the believer — Jesus. Let's preach until everyone is fully conscious of who he or she is in Christ, and has realized and released the full power of Christ through their lives. That is what we are to preach about.

To this [end] I also labor, striving according to His working which works in me mightily (Col. 1:29).

"See, Jesus, I knew Paul would slip and say that **you labored.** There still is self-effort which we are to put into this equation in order to make it work."

"Yes, Mark, but you missed the rest of Paul's sentence. He said I labor, '**striving according to His working which works in me mightily.**' "

"I guess Paul did say that, didn't he? Let's see... So you are not laboring according to your own personal strength at all?"

"That's right, Mark! You are laboring according to the power of the One who flows within you."

"Right. And how did you say you sensed this flow?"

"It is a Spirit flow, an inner quickening. It is sensed as a river of peace and power welling up within you."

"You actually feel it?"

"Of course. It feels like love, joy, peace, patience, faith, hope. One of the words for power is *energis* and it means active energy. It feels like a flow of active energy within you. It lifts your heaviness, and doubt and fear, and simply supernaturally washes them away. Every time you call on God to do that, He just does it."

"Jesus, you mean to say it's as simple as that?"

"Yes!"

"But don't you have to strive, or work at it, or something?"

"Well, yes, Mark, you do strive to enter into rest. But once you are at rest and no longer exerting your own strength, then out through your stillness the flow takes over."

"Interesting..."

For I want you to know what a **great conflict** I have for you and those in Laodicea, and [for] as many as have not seen my face in the flesh, **that their hearts may be encouraged, being knit together in love, and [attaining] to all riches of the full assurance of understanding, to the knowledge of the mystery of God,** both of the Father and of Christ, in whom are hidden all the treasures of wisdom and knowledge (Col. 2:1-3).

"You see, Mark, one wars so that people's hearts may be encouraged."

"That's interesting. I used to like to hit people, in Christian love, so I could get them to repent..."

"Mark, I want to knit them in love, and into a confident understanding and experience of the oneness they now experience with Christ, who flows effortlessly out through their hearts. In this flow is everything they will ever need. Therefore, if they can learn to become attuned to this flow as they walk through life, they can have supernatural wisdom, and supernatural might and supernatural....you name it."

"Awesome! I guess my preaching should center upon touching this Divine flow within the heart of the believer?"

"Now you've got it!"

For though I am absent in the flesh, yet I am with you in spirit, rejoicing to see your [good] order and the steadfastness of your faith in Christ (Col. 2:5).

"There, Lord, I knew you wanted me to focus on ordering my life and making it steadfast. I am going back to preaching about steadfastness."

"Mark, you missed the last half of the sentence again. The steadfastness that one celebrates is **steadfastness of faith in Christ,** and what He is and does within the heart of the believer."

"Oh. Okay."

"Mark, what I really want you to preach about is being a steadfast believer in the might and power of Christ to overcome all odds and establish His Kingdom in and through the hearts of men."

"But if I preach about faith all the time, I might end up sounding like Schuller or one of those faith teachers."

"Would that be so bad? Didn't we agree that the abiding realities were faith, hope and love (I Cor. 13:13)?"

"Yes, I guess we did. You mean I am supposed to preach about these three things continuously?"

"They are the heart of the Kingdom."

"Hmmm..."

As you have therefore received Christ Jesus the Lord, so walk in Him (Col. 2:6).

"Mark, how did you receive Jesus Christ?"

"I fought my way through all the intellectual obstacles, and uncertainties, and then I..."

"No, you didn't. An angel kept whispering in your ear the same phrase over and over again until you couldn't resist any longer and you succumbed to My convicting power."

"Yes, I guess that may be closer to the true story."

"You see, Mark, you received Christ Jesus the Lord through simple faith, a faith I put within your heart, and you allowed that faith to flow, simply believing that I had done all, and all you needed to do was accept My atoning work of salvation. Now I want you to exercise that same faith as you walk through life. Don't try to do things on your own. I am the Alpha and the Omega, the Beginning and the End, the First and the Last. When you need anything at all, look within to Me, the One who lives within your heart and spirit, the One who gives graciously to those who ask. Do not turn to your own strength. You were not saved through your own strength. You cannot keep yourself through your own strength. Therefore, come to Me and I will heal you and establish you upon a mighty hill, a hill called Mount Zion."

Rooted and built up in Him and established in the faith, as you have been taught, abounding in it with thanksgiving (Col. 2:7).

"You see, Mark, the establishment you need is not in works or self-effort. The establishing you need is in the effortless flow of My faith that wells up within your heart as a stream of living water, and transforms you from the inside. That is what you need. Come, be established in My flow. Come, My son."

"Yes, my Lord, I come...to You."

"My son, all you really have to do in life is worship Me for the fulness of all things. I am all and in all, I am the first and the last. I am your life and your breath. Therefore, your activity is to abound with thanksgiving, rather than strife and sweat. Do you see that?"

"Yes, my Lord."

Beware lest anyone cheat you through philosophy and empty deceit, according to the tradition of men, according to the basic principles of the world, and not according to Christ. For in Him dwells all the fullness of the Godhead bodily; and you are complete in Him, who is the head of all principality and power. In Him you were also circumcised with the circumcision made without hands, by putting off the body of the sins of the flesh, by the circumcision of Christ, buried with Him in baptism, in which you also were raised with [Him] through faith in the working of God, who raised Him from the dead (Col. 2:8-12).

"Mark, many will come, saying, 'Do this,' and 'Do that,' and 'Try this,' and 'Try that'. However, do not be deceived. Christianity is Me and only Me. It is not rules and principles. It is not techniques and theologies. It is a Person: Me. It is Me, loving you, loving the whole world through you. That is what Christianity is. Many will seek to make it many other things. However, it is not other things. It is Me loving you, Me loving them. That is what Christianity is. Do not be drawn into deception, My son."

"Yes, my Lord."

"And concerning your heart. When it needs help, I am there to help it. When it needs evil cut out of it, I am there to circumcise it. No man can heal the heart. Only I can. That is why My success rate in healing hurting individuals will always be far above man's, because no man can heal the heart. The heart belongs to the Lord. It is mine, says the Lord of Hosts."

Therefore let no one judge you in food or in drink, or regarding a festival or a new moon or sabbaths, which are a shadow of things to come, but the substance is of Christ. Let no one defraud you of your reward, taking delight in [false] humility and worship of angels, intruding into those things which he has not seen, vainly puffed up by his fleshly mind, and not holding fast to the Head, from whom all the body, nourished and knit together by joints and ligaments, grows with the increase [which is] from God. Therefore, if you died with Christ from the basic principles of the world, why, as [though] living in the world, do you subject yourselves to regulations — "Do not touch, do not taste, do not handle," which all concern things which perish with the using — according to the commandments and doctrines of men? These things indeed have an appearance of wisdom in self imposed religion, [false] humility, and neglect of the body, [but are] of no value against the indulgence of the flesh (Col. 2:16-23).

"Mark, the reason I have written this warning is that I know many will relegate Christianity to this level, even though this is not what I have made. This is what man has made. This is the counterpart to true Christianity. This is the counterfeit. It is full of rules and regulations, and 'touch nots,' and 'taste nots.' However, this is the surface, and I deal with the heart. Yes, the surface is important, but only as an outworking of that which is in the heart. To tackle the surface has no value in healing the heart. To heal the heart will also heal the surface. Therefore, we do not give attention to the surface. Not because it is not important. Indeed it is. However, it is a by-product of that which is much deeper — the heart of man.

Therefore, you and I will focus on the heart; how to heal the heart and how to release My power through man's heart, because in doing that we shall do all things. Behold, I have spoken. I shall bring it to pass. Thus says the Lord of Hosts."

Set your mind on things above, not on things on the earth. For you died, and your life is hidden with Christ in God. When Christ [who is] our life appears, then you also will appear with Him in glory (Col. 3:2-4).

"Now, Mark, we will set our minds on things above, on spiritual things. We will not focus on earthly things. We will focus on spiritual powers and principalities and angels and demons, and the growth of My kingdom which is by faith. That is what we will study. That is what we will discuss. That is what we will preach. That is what we will teach. And in so doing, we will heal the hearts of man. In so doing, we will heal the kingdoms of this world. Are they not all in My hand? Yes, My son, they are. From the smallest heart to the greatest kingdom, they are in My hand. Therefore, we shall heal them, because we shall set our minds on the things of the Spirit. Mark, preach on My Spirit and teach on My Spirit. That is your commission. That is your lifeline. There is no life outside of My Spirit. Come to My Spirit, My child, and you shall be transformed. Come, and again I say, come."

"Now when you look at the laws in the second half of Colossians they will appear very differently. No longer will they be rules that you obey through the strength of your might. No, now they shall be commandments that I obey through the strength of My might as I live My life through you. Now they are My commands which are kept by My power. You are simply one through whom another flows. However, you are not simple. I have made you very complex. And I have made you special. There is none like you. Each of My children has been specially fashioned by My hand. So each of you is special. Each of you is Mine. Go, My son, in peace."

"Yes, my Lord."

A Review of Some Key Points from Chapter Twelve

☐ The central dynamic of New Testament Christianity is an inner growing relationship with the Lord Jesus Christ.

☐ Once one has a revelation of the central dynamic of Christianity, the entire New Testament takes on new meaning.

☐ The commands of the New Testament are only to be viewed in light of the abiding reality of Christ our life.

☐ It is Christ who keeps these commands through us. It is not us keeping them. We can't keep them because they are supernatural and we in our own flesh are natural.

☐ We must learn to allow God to speak to us as we read the New Testament. We must pray for a "spirit of revelation," that the eyes of our hearts be enlightened...that we may know (Eph. 1:17,18).

☐ List other points that were important to you from this chapter.

Think and Discuss

☐ What is your response to the above example of Bible study? If you noticed, we began by meditating on the text. We then progressed to dialoguing with God, the ultimate Author of the text. Is this what Bible study is supposed to be (Eph. 1:17,18)? Have you ever done this in your Bible study? Why not try it with one of the passages recommended below?

☐ Meditate on other passages from the New Testament, and see if in light of the study of the truths of this book they don't appear entirely new also. Try Galatians 3,4,5; Ephesians 1-5; Philippians 1-4. Try the method of meditation exemplified in this chapter and discussed in point one above. See what the experience is like for you. You may want to add a week or two to this course as each of the members of your group goes home and works through the above suggested portions of Scripture with your journal at your side. Then come back together and share what the Lord has revealed to you!

☐ Enter a Bible passage as a group, allowing God to speak to you through the passage. You may choose any passage. One possibility would be to join the disciples as they waited in the upper room for the day of Pentecost. As a group, you may want to reread the historical narrative (Acts 1:4-13; Acts 1:21-2:4). Then sit in a circle, join hands, and corporately enter into the story, with each person sharing what they are feeling or sensing as they go deep into their hearts and meet Christ there. Each person may share for a minute or two and then squeeze the hand of the person on their right, as a signal that they are done and the next can take their turn. If a person wants to pass, he simply squeezes the hand of the person on his right. When it is your turn to share, you may share what your heart is experiencing, what the Lord is saying to you, what you are seeing, your fears or concerns, or your faith and hopes. You may speak forth the dialogue that is going on between you and the Lord. Corporately you can enter into the story, meet Christ and be transformed by the encounter. Don't be afraid to try this new adventure. Try it, you may find you like it.

☐ **Journaling** — "Lord, talk to me about what true Bible study is to be like. Is it what I have been doing? Are there any ways You want my process of Bible study to deepen? If so, how? Thank You, Lord, for what You say." Write the above questions in your journal and record what the Lord responds. Come prepared to share it in class.

Chapter Thirteen

A New Theological Box or The Experience of Divine Encounter?

Finally we have finished this part of my life's story. We have discovered seven new truths:

Truth # 1 — God is all and in all.

Truth # 2 — I am a vessel.

Truth # 3 — I no longer live.

Truth # 4 — Christ is my life.

Truth # 5 — I am dead to the Law.

Truth # 6 — I live by the Spirit (tuned to *rhema* and *vision*).

Truth # 7 — I live by faith that God is Immanuel.

Maybe we should build a new theology around these seven truths. My old theology was what I would characterize as a "worm theology." You know, the idea that man is a worm. And

I could back it up with Scripture: "Thou worm, Jacob." Maybe we could call this new theology "union life," or "living the replaced life," or...something like that. What do you think?

Do I really want to create a new theology? Maybe life isn't in theologies, anyway. Maybe it is in a stream, a river, a flow. Maybe I don't need to precisely, theologically define and delineate the truths of this book. Maybe what we have here is a new experience (or at least a deepened one) in the Holy Spirit.

If I degenerate the truths of this book into a theology, I run into the danger of saying, "We are fused to God, and therefore everything we say or do is God, so listen up, this is God talking." Youch! Not good. This is not exactly what I had in mind as the end result of this book. Much closer would be the one who has established great meekness in his life because he realizes that he is dust fused to Glory. He always remains the dust. God always remains the Glory. That is my picture as I walk through life: I am dust fused to Glory. That way, I always know who I am, I always know who God is, and I always know who the two of us are when we are fused together (I Cor. 6:17).

So, instead of saying we have a new theology, let's say we have learned to encounter God more deeply and live out of Him more thoroughly than ever before. I like that much better, don't you?

To complete this book and to emphasize the point that this is not a new theology, but a deepened relationship, I thought I might share some of my journaling with you from the last year or two. It is not all necessarily on the seven truths of this book, because when God and I sit down and talk, we talk about a lot of things. Life isn't always nicely compartmentalized into seven little truths. Life just is. So bear with me as I share some of my wonder of Divine encounter with you.

10-30-89

Good morning, Jesus. What would You like to speak to me this day?

Mark, I need you to come to Me daily during this period of your life. There is so much change. There is so much going on that you need to hear a fresh word from Me daily if you are to be sustained and kept on track.

All right, Lord, I will seek by Your grace to do that.

Now, concerning today. You have already heard Me as you have gone jogging. I have given you this time to set up your office and rewrite your books and have them produced professionally. Do not worry. When the time comes to print them, you will have the money. I shall supply it. However, now is the time to complete those tasks. Much hangs in the balance. Do not be sluggish, but know what the will of God is and do the will of God. All other things shall fall into place. Watch and see the salvation of the Lord.

What else?

Mark, love your wife...Love your wife and children.

Thank you, Lord.

11-1-89

I woke up from a dream:

I was running a race in a mountainous area. Wind was blowing hard against me, keeping me afloat. The wind died down. The way narrowed to a narrow ledge. I began to crawl. Then fear took over. I stopped and began to panic. One came up behind me, leapt to a ledge above me and swept down some hay chaff. Then he jumped. It was so far down, I was sure he would hurt or kill himself. He landed softly and sprang up, encouraging me to do the same. I was afraid and began to crawl back, prepared to look for another way. He pulled the bales out from under me and down I tumbled. Fear struck my heart. Then I landed softly without hurting myself. I had made it!

Journaled Interpretation

> Mark, fear has brought you to a standstill. Rebuke the fear and leap into the unknown. I am there to catch you. I have gone before you and prepared the way.

Yes, Lord. Is there any special action I am supposed to take?

> Yes. Aggressively love your wife and children. They need your mind and heart.....

11-25-89

Lord, what about finances?

> Mark, have I not taken care of you thus far? Will I not continue to take care of You? Of course, My child. Why do you worry? If I so arrayed the birds of the air, will I not care also for you?

Lord, so much I have done seems so in vain.

> You are right, My child, because you are operating out of fear and presumption. Do you not know that man's ways are not God's ways? Do not devise your own plan, but wait upon Me. Do not be anxious for tomorrow, for tomorrow will have enough care of its own. Each day has its own problems. Focus on the needs of today. Focus on the call of today.

Well, Lord, what is the call of today?

> To get your books finalized. To become successful in... To get your corporations and operations set up. That is the work of today. To love your family and quit pushing so hard. Has all your pushing accomplished anything? No, nothing. Again I say unto you, nothing. Watch and see the salvation of the Lord. Watch, I say, and see the salvation of the Lord.

12-11-89

Good morning, Jesus. I have no idea what activities are important to You this day. Please share what I am to be doing.

Well, son, the most important activity is to get a nice Christmas tree for your family and help them with the setup. That is very important to Patti. Therefore, that is very important to you. It is a great family activity. Make it one.

Yes, Lord.

12-12-89

Good morning, Lord. Please breathe new life upon Patti and me. We need Your healing power this day.

Yes, Mark, I know. Now that you have asked, I will supply.

Lord, bring into our lives the people and provision which You have planned for us.

I shall, My son. Watch and see the salvation of the Lord.

Lord, is it premature to begin working on the Lifelong Curriculum Catalog?

No, My son, you may begin now.

12-7-89

Mark, why do you rush down these paths of your own choosing without first consulting Me? Do you not consider this a major decision? Do you not feel it is worthy to hear My input on this matter, much less submit it to authority?

Yes, Lord, I suppose You are right. What would You like to say to me?

Well, first of all, this was not My idea. It came to you but not from Me. Therefore, it will avail nothing. Do not invest money in it because it will return you no profit. I shall be your Source. I shall provide for you. Do not trust on the arm of the flesh to provide the supernatural provision of Almighty

God. It is God Himself who shall provide for your needs. It is God Himself who shall be glorified.

Do you not know that we are building a story, you and I? We are working together on a travelogue of story and faith. This is an important story that is being built. That is why I am watching over it so closely. I am not allowing it to get off track. You can get this line of credit this day, however, I do not want you to. I will be your provision. Wait and you shall see the salvation of the Lord. You shall not have to jeopardize your home or your lifestyle for that which I have called you to. I shall provide supernaturally. You are not to pursue this loan at this time.

Okay, Lord.

Simply do the banking that is to be done and work on the things I have set before you.

Yes, Lord.

2-20-90

Mark, today mighty decisions are being made that will affect your future in great ways. Today is to be a day of prayer and worship of Me. Today you are to give in its entirety to Me as a sacrifice of the fruit of your lips. It is not a day of writing. It is not a day of study. It is a day of prayer, that I will move mountains in people's hearts, that I will do mighty and wondrous things. Today is a day of prayer for both ..... and for ..... They all need your prayer. Today is a day of prayer and fasting before Me. Seek My face in a mighty way this day, My son, and watch and behold the miracles that I will perform on your behalf.

Do only that which is necessary. Let the rest wait for another day, My son. Watch and see the salvation of the Lord. Watch, I say, and see the salvation of the Lord.

Yes, Lord, strengthen and lead me this day, I pray.

I will, My son, only come to Me. I will.

2-23-90

> Mark, it should be clear to you that satan is attacking you. Resist him and he will flee from you. Stand firm in Me and I shall sustain you.

Strengthen me, my Lord.

> Mark, I shall help you this day. It shall be an anointed day of writing and activities. Enjoy it and Me. Go to work. There are many things we are going to do this day.

Life goes on. Each day there is a new adventure with the Lord. Each day is a step of faith as I walk out into the unknown, trusting the flow from my heart. Yes, it is risky living. Yes, I even make mistakes from time to time. However, it is the best way of living I have discovered thus far in my life. From all I can tell, it is the way the prophets in the Bible lived. From what I can sense, this is a way of releasing the Divine power of Almighty God through our hearts. I recommend it to you. And if you fall, I encourage you to do the same thing I do. Get back up and say, "God, can we try again?" I am sure after we have walked in this for a generation or two we will be much more skilled as a culture in walking with God. In the meantime, we must start where we are and go from there. I know of no other way.

May God's richest blessing be upon your life as you travel the road of life **naturally supernatural!**

Review of Some Key Points from Chapter Thirteen

☐ The goal of this book is not the establishment of a new theology.

☐ Life is not to be a theology, but to be simply "life".

☐ The goal of this book is that we have a deepened experience with God, not a new theology.

☐ We should just let life be a growing, dynamic, ongoing encounter with Almighty God, rather than bits and pieces of theology.

☐ For me, all that I have said boils down to journaling and Divine encounter on a daily basis. That is life to me. That is how I live out the truths of this book. That is how I recommend that you live out the truths of this book.

Think and Discuss

☐ Why are we so prone to turn new insights into new theologies? Is this wise? Is this expedient? Is this necessary? Is there any detriment in turning a new experience with God into a new theology? If so, what is the detriment?

☐ Is theology head-focused or heart-focused? Is theology life or an overlay on life? Should Christians focus on experiencing God in life, or on a theology about God? Where have you spent most of your energies as a Christian?

☐ Does theology unite or divide the Church? Can we test a thing by its fruit? If theology divides the Church, can we say the fruit of emphasizing it is bad? Or would it be better to say that "I" have the right theology and the other 2300 denominations in Christianity are wrong? What do you think?

☐ Did Jesus emphasize theology or did He simply manifest the power of God in the experiences of life? Did He tend to eradicate theology with His simple yet profound sayings, "But I say unto you..."? What drew people to Jesus?

☐ **Journaling** — Write the following questions on the top of a page in your journal: "Lord, would you please talk to me about the truths of this book, and how they relate to theology? Is there value in theology? If so, what is it? Is there danger in theology? If so, what is it?" Record the answer He gives you. Come prepared to share it with your small group.

Appendix A

You Can Hear God's Voice

The age in which we live is so married to rationalism and cognitive, analytical thought that we almost mock when we hear of one actually claiming to be able to hear the voice of God. However, we must not mock for several reasons. First, men and women throughout the Bible heard God's voice. Also, there are some highly effective and reputable men and women of God alive today who demonstrate that they hear God's voice. Finally, there is a deep hunger within us all to commune with God, and to hear Him speak within our hearts.

As a Bible-believing, born-again Christian, I struggled unsuccessfully for years to hear God's voice. I prayed, fasted, studied my Bible and listened for a voice within, all to no avail. **There was no inner voice that I could hear!** Then God set me aside for a year to study, read, and experiment in the area of learning to hear God's voice. During that time God taught me **four keys that opened the door to two-way prayer.** I have discovered that not only do they work for me, but they have worked for many thousands of Christians who have been taught to use them. Actually, 99 percent of those whom I have taught have broken through into two-way dialogue with God, bringing tremendous intimacy to their Christian experience and transforming their very way of living. This will happen to you also as you seek God, utilizing the following four keys. They are all found in Habakkuk 2:1,2. I encourage you to read this passage before going on.

Key # 1 — God's voice in our hearts sounds like a flow of spontaneous thoughts. Therefore, when I tune to God, I tune to spontaneity.

The Bible says, "The Lord answered me and said...."(Hab. 2:2) Habakkuk knew the sound of God's voice. The Bible describes it as a still, small voice. I had always listened for an inner **audible** voice, and surely God can and does speak that way at times. However, I have found that for most of us, most of the time, God's inner voice comes to us as **spontaneous thoughts, visions, feelings, or impressions**. For example, haven't each of us had the experience of driving down the road and having **a thought come to us** to pray for a certain person? We generally acknowledge this as the voice of God urging us to pray for that individual. My question to you is, "What did God's voice sound like as you drove in your car?" Was it an inner, audible voice, or was it a spontaneous thought that lit upon your mind? Most of you would say that God's voice came to you as a spontaneous thought.

So I thought to myself, "Maybe when I listen for God's voice, I should be listening for a flow of spontaneous thoughts. Maybe spirit level communication is received as spontaneous thoughts, impressions, feelings, and visions." Through experimentation and feedback from thousands of others, I am now convinced that this is so.

The Bible confirms this in many ways. The definition of *paga*, the Hebrew word for intercession, is "a chance encounter" or "an accidental intersecting." Therefore, as God lays people on our hearts for intercession, He does it through *paga*, a chance encounter thought "accidentally" intersecting our thought processes. Therefore, when I tune to God, I tune to chance encounter thoughts or spontaneous thoughts. When I am poised quietly before God in prayer, I have found that the flow of spontaneous thoughts that comes is quite definitely from God.

Key # 2 — I must learn to still my own thoughts and emotions, so that I can sense God's flow of thoughts and emotions within me.

Habakkuk said, "I will stand my watch and set myself on the rampart..."(Hab. 2:l) Habakkuk knew that in order to hear God's quiet, inner, spontaneous thoughts, he first had to go to a quiet place and still his own thoughts and emotions. Psalm 46:l0 encourages us to "Be still, and know that I am God." There is a deep inner knowing (spontaneous flow) in our spirit that each of us can experience when we quiet our flesh and our minds.

I have found several simple ways to quiet myself so that I can more readily pick up God's spontaneous flow. Loving God through a quiet worship song is a most effective means for many (note II Kings 3:15). It is as I become still (thoughts, will, and emotions) and am poised before God that the Divine flow is realized. Therefore, after I worship quietly and become still, I open myself for that spontaneous flow. If thoughts come to me of things I have forgotten to do, I write them down and then dismiss them. If thoughts of guilt or unworthiness come to my mind, I repent thoroughly, receive the washing of the blood of the Lamb, and put on His robe of righteousness, seeing myself spotless before the presence of God.

As I fix my gaze upon Jesus (Heb. 12:2), becoming quiet in His presence, and sharing with Him what is on my heart, I find that two-way dialogue begins to flow. Spontaneous thoughts flow from the throne of God to me, and I find that I am actually conversing with the King of kings.

It is very important that you become still and properly focused if you are going to receive the pure word of God. If you are not still, you will simply be receiving your own thoughts. If you are not properly focused on Jesus, you will receive an impure flow, because the intuitive flow comes out of that upon which you have fixed your eyes. Therefore, if you fix your eyes upon Jesus, the intuitive flow comes from Jesus. If you fix your gaze upon some desire of your heart, the intuitive flow comes out of that desire of your heart. To have a pure flow, you must first "become still," and second, you must carefully "fix your eyes upon Jesus." Again I will say, this is quite easily accomplished by quietly worshiping the King, and then receiving out of the stillness that follows.

Key # 3 — As I pray, I fix the eyes of my heart upon Jesus, seeing in the Spirit the dreams and visions of Almighty God.

We have already alluded to this principle in the previous paragraphs; however, we need to develop it a bit further. Habakkuk said, "I will keep watch to see," and God said, "Record the vision" (Hab. 2:1,2). It is very interesting that Habakkuk was going to actually start looking for vision as he prayed. He was going to open the eyes of his heart, and look into the spirit world to see what God wanted to show him. This is an intriguing idea.

I had never thought of opening the eyes of my heart and looking for vision. However, the more I thought of it, the more I realized this was exactly what God intends me to do. He gave me eyes in my heart. They are not to be used for lust, or to visualize failure. They are to be used to see in the spirit world the vision and movement of Almighty God. I believe there is an active spirit world functioning all around me. This world is full of angels, demons, the Holy Spirit, the omnipresent God, and His omnipresent Son, Jesus. There is no reason for me not to see it — other than my rational culture, which tells me not to believe it is even there and provides no instructions on how to become open to seeing this spirit world.

The most obvious prerequisite to seeing is that we need **to look**. Daniel was seeing a vision **in his mind** and he said, "I was looking...I kept looking...I kept looking" (Dan. 7:1,9,13). As I pray, I look for Jesus present with me, and I watch Him as He speaks to me, doing and saying the things that are on His heart. Many Christians will find that if they will only look, they will see. Jesus is Emmanuel, God with us. It is as simple as that. You will see a spontaneous inner vision in much the same way you receive spontaneous inner thoughts. You can see Christ present with you in a comfortable setting, **because Christ** *is present with you in a comfortable setting*. Actually, you will discover that inner vision comes so easily you will have a tendency to reject it, thinking that it is just you. (Doubt is satan's most effective weapon against the Church.) However, if you will persist in recording these visions, your doubt will soon be overcome by faith, as you recognize that the content of them could only be birthed in Almighty God.

God continually revealed Himself to His covenant people through dream and vision. He did so from Genesis to Revelation and said that, since the Holy Spirit was poured out in Acts chapter two, we should expect to receive a continuing flow of dreams and visions (Acts 2:1-4). Jesus, our perfect example, demonstrated this ability of living out of ongoing contact with Almighty God. He said that He did nothing on His own initiative, but only that which He **saw the Father doing, and heard the Father saying** (John 5:19,20,30). What an incredible way to live!

Is it actually possible for us to live out of the Divine initiative as Jesus did? I believe it is. A major purpose of Jesus' death and resurrection was that the veil in the temple that divided the people from God be torn from top to bottom, giving us access into the immediate presence of God, and we are commanded to draw near (Heb. 10:19-22). Therefore, even though what I am describing seems a bit unusual to a rational twentieth-century culture, it is demonstrated and described as being a **central biblical teaching and experience.** It is time to restore to the Church that which belongs to the Church.

Because of their intense rational nature and existence in an overly rational culture, some will need more assistance and understanding of these truths before they can move into them. They will find this help in the book *Dialogue With God* by the same author.

Key # 4 — Journaling, the writing out of our prayers and God's answers, provides great freedom in hearing God's voice.

God told Habakkuk, "Write the vision and make it plain on tablets..." (Hab. 2:2). It had never crossed my mind to write out my prayers and God's answers as Habakkuk did. Actually, this was commanded by God. If you begin to search Scripture for this idea, you will find hundreds of chapters demonstrating it (Psalms, many of the prophets, Revelation). Why then hadn't I ever thought of it? Why hadn't I ever heard a sermon on it?

I decided to call the process journaling, and I began to experiment with it. I discovered it was a fabulous facilitator to clearly discerning God's inner spontaneous flow, because as I journaled I was able **to write in faith for long periods of time,** simply believing it was God. I did not have to test it as I was receiving it (which jams one's receiver), because I knew that when the flow was over I could go back and test and examine it carefully **at that time,** making sure that it lined up with Scripture.

You will be amazed as you attempt journaling. Doubt may hinder you at first, but throw it off, reminding yourself that it is a biblical concept, and that God is present, speaking to His children. Don't take yourself too seriously. When you do, you become tense and get in the way of the Holy Spirit's movement. It is when we cease **our labors** and enter His rest that God is free to flow (Heb. 4:10). Therefore, put a smile on your face, sit back comfortably, get out your pen and paper, and turn your attention toward God in praise and worship, seeking His face. As you write out your question to God and become still, fixing your gaze on Jesus, who is present with you, you will suddenly have a very good thought in response to your question. Don't doubt it, simply write it down. Later as you go over your journaling, you, too, will be amazed to discover that you are indeed dialoguing with God.

Some final notes. No one should attempt this without having first read through at least the New Testament (preferably the entire Bible), nor should one attempt this unless he is submitted to solid spiritual leadership. All major directional moves that come through journaling should be submitted before being acted upon. It is *highly recommended* that before pursuing the techniques described above, the reader more thoroughly acquaint himself with them by reading the entire book *Communion With God* or *Dialogue With God* by the same author. May the experience of Habakkuk be yours!

Communion With God —
The Package of Materials

This is the most practical, down-to-earth training available today on how Christians can dialogue with God. Over 99 percent of all participants begin to write down many pages of dialogue with Almighty God on a regular basis. If you are not completely satisfied with this material and do not personally begin to hear and record the things the Lord is speaking to you, you may return this material in resalable condition within 30 days for a full money back refund.

Communion With God Student's Workbook — a 224-page "write-in" study manual. Mark teaches through this text on both the video and audio cassettes. $15.95

Communion With God Teacher's Guide — Twenty-four session outlines corresponding to the 24 video and audio sessions, laying the course out in detail for the leader/teacher. $13.95

Communion With God Video Tapes — Twenty-four half-hour sessions of Mark Virkler teaching Communion With God . $199.95

Communion With God Audio Cassettes — Twenty-four half-hour sessions of Mark Virkler teaching in a classroom setting. $35.95

Dialogue With God — a 250-page teaching testimonial sharing not only the teaching of Communion With God, but also many pages of inspiring stories and testimonies. Included are 30 pages of journaling from individuals across several nations — a great source of encouragement for those beginning to journal. $8.95

My Adventures with God: A Journal — More than merely a notebook of lined paper, this journal also includes a review of the four keys to hearing God's voice, what to do if your journaling is wrong, tips to overcoming stumbling blocks and a place for your own personal table of contents. Each journal page has a verse at the top providing instruction, support and encouragement in your spiritual walk. $8.95

Counseled By God —
The Package of Materials

A revolutionary book showing you plainly how you can find healing for the basic emotional needs of your life by dialoguing through them with God. It deals with such topics as healing anger, fear, inferiority and condemnation; allowing Christ to heal deep hurts from the past; and learning to incubate only God's voice and vision. If you have found the deep healing that comes as this book has guided you into interaction with God, you may want to obtain other supporting materials for either your personal use or group use.

Counseled by God Textbook — a 115-page stand alone trade paperback. Excellent for personal use. $7.95

Counseled by God Student Workbook — a 100-page "write-in" study manual. Excellent for group use. Mark Virkler teaches through this text on both video and audio cassettes. $9.95

Counseled by God Teacher's Guide — Twenty-two lesson outlines corresponding to the 22 video and audio sessions, laying the course out in detail for the leader/teacher. 10.95

Counseled by God Video Tapes — Eleven hours of Mark Virkler teaching in a classroom setting. $199.95

Counseled by God Audio Cassettes - Eleven hours of Mark Virkler teaching in a classroom setting. $35.95

Mark Virkler is available as a seminar speaker. He travels full time conducting Communion With God and other seminars at churches worldwide. Contact him at 716-652-6990 to make arrangements to have him come to your church.

Cultivating Individual and Corporate Creativity — The Package of Materials

These texts restore the entrepreneur spirit to the Church of Jesus Christ. The goal of the Christian life is not simply death to the flesh, but a release of the resurrection power of Almighty God in every sphere and domain of life. This package deals with these themes.

Spirit Born Creativity: Releasing God's Creativity into Your World — The only book of its kind, teaching the process of releasing the creativity of God through the heart of the believer. Ideal for businessmen, parents and anyone who wants to become more creative. It shows step by step how one releases the creativity of Almighty God by filling all five senses to become more creative. It shows step by step how one releases the creativity of Almighty God by filling all five senses of his spirit with God's spoken word and vision. This 238-page trade size paperback by Mark and Patti Virkler sells for $9.95. Teacher's guide available — $5.95.

What the Bible Says About Silver and Gold — Have you noticed that Abraham, Isaac, David, Solomon and others were both spiritual leaders in their communities and multi-millionaires? Did you realize you could be both? Does God want to release the wealth of the world to His children? What do we need to learn so we will be ready and able to handle it? How is it released? Does it float out of the sky or do we work and plan and pray and then see the fulfillment of our labors? This booklet by Mark and Patti Virkler covers verses from Scripture on these topics. $4.95

Twenty Key Biblical Principles for Christian Management — Whether you are responsible for the management for a church or a business, you need to conduct yourself according to God's principles. Included are 20 evaluation pages for you to evaluate yourself according to the 20 key biblical principles of management. 110-page manual

These texts restore the entrepreneur spirit to the Church of Jesus Christ. The goal of the Christian life is not simply death to the flesh, but a release of the resurrection power of Almighty God in every sphere and domain of life. This package deals with these themes.

Spirit Born Creativity: Releasing God's Creativity into Your World — The only book of its kind, teaching the process of releasing the creativity of God through the heart of the believer. Ideal for business-men, parents and anyone who wants to become more creative. It shows step by step how one releases the creativity of Almighty God by filling all five senses to become more creative. It shows step by step how one releases the creativity of Almighty God by filling all five senses of his spirit with God's spoken word and vision. This 238-page trade size paperback by Mark and Patti Virkler sells for $9.95. Teacher's guide available — $5.95.

What the Bible Says About Silver and Gold — Have you noticed that Abraham, Isaac, David, Solomon and others were both spiritual leaders in their communities and multi-millionaires? Did you realize you could be both? Does God want to release the wealth of the world to His children? What do we need to learn so we will be ready and able to handle it? How is it released? Does it float out of the sky or do we work and plan and pray and then see the fulfillment of our labors? This booklet by Mark and Patti Virkler covers verses from Scripture on these topics. $4.95

Twenty Key Biblical Principles for Christian Management — Whether you are responsible for the management for a church or a business, you need to conduct yourself according to God's principles. Included are 20 evaluation pages for you to evaluate yourself according to the 20 key biblical principles of management. 110-page manual by Mark and Patti Virkler $9.95.

Go Natural!
Eden's Health Plan

Live Long Enough to Fulfill Your Destiny!

by Mark & Patti Virkler

> "The doctor of the future will give no medicine, but will interest his patient in the care of the human frame, in diet and in the cause and prevention of disease."
>
> *Thomas A. Edison*

Learn how to:
- Live longer & healthier
- Live with more vitality
- Remove cancer through diet
- Reduce or remove arthritis
- Permanently lose unwanted fat
- Remove all risk of heart disease
- Overcome osteoporosis &diabetes

This book is for you if you:
- are sick and tired of being sick and tired,
- are seeking to glorify God in your body,
- want to live longer with more health and vitality.

This book can save your life!
- Discover the amazing correlation between biblical injunctions on diet and health, and the most recent scientific research.
- Take charge of your own health and discover how to keep yourself young, vivacious, attractive and free of degenerative diseases.

Learn how to overcome sickness and degenerative diseases by:
- Detoxifying your body
- Rebuilding your immune system
- Nourishing your body's cells

"Behold I have set before you this day life and death...
Choose life..." (Deut. 30:19)

Publications of Communion With God Ministries
1431 Bullis Rd., Elma, N.Y. 14059   Office Phone 1-716-652-6990
Order Line 1-800-466-6961   Fax 1-716-652-6961

Name_____Phone _____

Address_____

#	TITLE	UNIT PRICE	EXTENDED COST
	Go Natural! – Eden's Health Plan - Virkler	$12.95	
	Go Natural! Student's Workbook - Virkler	$ 6.95	
	Go Natural! Teacher's Guide - Virkler	$14.95	
	Go Natural! Video Cassettes 6 hours of Mark Virkler teaching though the book	$99.00	
	Go Natural! Audio Cassettes 6 hours of Mark Virkler teaching though the book	$19.95	
COMMUNION WITH GOD SERIES Teaching people to hear God's voice and see His vision. This WILL bring you into the experience of two-way dialogue with God.			
	200 page student's workbook	$17.95	
	100 page teacher's guide	$13.95	
	Dialogue With God	$8.95	
	Dialoguing With God Review Booklet	$2.95	
	Learning to Communicate With God (A teen adaptation)	$7.95	
	Corporate Communion With God	$4.95	
	My Adventures With God - A Journal	$8.95	
	Learning to Hear God's Voice - Riffel	$7.95	
	Our Father Speaks Through Hebrews - Lord	$9.95	
	Talking With Jesus (Devotional)	$8.95	
	Seduction?? A Biblical Response	$7.95	
	You Can Hear God's Voice (tract)	$ .10	
	Overcoming Blocks & Hindrances to Hearing God's Voice (tract)	$ .10	
	New Age or New Birth pamphlet	$ .25	
	New Age versus Christianity cassettes	$3.95	
	New Age versus Christianity video	$14.95	
	Phariseeism versus Christianity cassettes	$3.95	
	Phariseeism versus Christianity video	$14.95	
	12 hrs of training cassettes (teaches the student workbook)	$34.95	
	12 hrs of training videos (teaches the student workbook)	$199.95	
	Journaling Organizer Software for the IBM	$49.00	

#	TITLE	UNIT PRICE	EXTENDED COST
COUNSELED BY GOD SERIES Jesus said, "My words are life." This course is unique in its training of Christians on how to heal life's emotional struggles through dialoguing with God. A unique and revolutionary approach that truly heals the human heart of anger, guilt, fear, inferiority, condemnation and depression. (Formerly titled "Pure in Heart").			
	100 page student's workbook	$9.95	
	80 page teacher's guide	$10.95	
	115 page textbook	$8.95	
	11 hours of training cassettes	$34.95	
	11 hours of training videos	$199.95	
CHRISTIAN DREAM INTERPRETATION Throughout the Bible, God has spoken through dreams and visions, and He is still doing so today. In typical Daniel-like fashion, you will learn to hear from God in this way, allowing Him to grant you the interpretation of your dreams.			
	Biblical Research Concerning Dreams & Visions - Virkler	$5.95	
	Biblical Research Concerning Dreams & Visions Teacher's Guide - Virkler	$5.95	
	Dreams: Wisdom Within - Riffel	$9.95	
	Christian Dream Interpretation Video Guide	$5.95	
	Christian Dream Interpretation video series	$99.95	
	Christian Dream Interpretation audio cassettes	$34.95	
CREATIVE MANAGEMENT SERIES Designed to cultivate individual and corporate creativity by releasing the Spirit's creativity, His creation and release of finance, and His anointed management.			
	Spirit Born Creativity text	$9.95	
	What the Bible Says about Silver and Gold	$4.95	
	Twenty Key Biblical Principles for Management	$9.95	
	Creative Management Seminar cassettes (5 hours)	$19.95	
	Creative Management Seminar videos (5 hours)	$69.95	
	Information on multi-level marketing opportunities	Free	
NATURALLY SUPERNATURAL This is a powerful revelation of the truth of Gal. 2:20 "I have been crucified with Christ; and it is no longer I who live, but Christ lives in me; and the life which I now live in the flesh I live by the faith of the Son of God."			
	The Foundations of Life	$9.95	
	Abiding in Christ	$13.95	
	Abiding in Christ Teacher's Guide	$12.95	
	The Anointing of the Holy Spirit - Peter Tan	$7.95	
	The Anointing of the Holy Spirit Workbook - Virkler	$4.95	

#	TITLE	UNIT PRICE	EXTENDED COST
	Abiding in Christ Part I - Cassettes (11 hours)	$34.95	
	Developing Heart Faith A practical study guide helping one move from head to "heart faith" through learning how to receive freshly spoken rhema and divinely generated visions.	$5.95	
	**TRANSMITTING SPIRIT LIFE IN THE CLASSROOM** A philosophical, theological, psychological and scientific backdrop for Holy Spirit encounter in our lives. Designed for the pastor and scholarly student, this intensive documentation offers full academic credibility to the belief that man can have direct and ongoing spiritual encounter with Almighty God, as he walks through life. It also discusses how Spirit life is transmitted in the classroom.		
	157 page Textbook	$14.95	
	47 page Booklet	$3.95	
	3 hours of training videos	$59.00	
	3 hours of training audio cassettes	$19.95	
	Experiencing God in the Small Group This book maintains that the small group should offer more than a teaching about God. The small group should offer experiences and encounters with God.	$10.95	
	Lamad Principles for Teachers	$10.95	
	Tools for the Workman An course designed to train one to do original Bible study utilizing the many Bible study resources available.	$10.95	
	Tools for the Workman Teacher's Guide	$10.95	
	**THE FIVE FOLD MINISTRY** Ephesians 4:11,12 lists the five fold ministry gifts. These materials are designed to help you establish 5-fold teams in your church and develop team leadership.		
	Dynamic Five Fold Team Leadership - Virkler	$10.95	
	Discovering Your Heart's Motivations & Ministry/Vocation Placement - Virkler	$14.95	
	Discovering My Dreams & Motivations (the personal profiles as found in the above book)	$5.00	
	The Five Fold Ministry — 3 Catalogs on how to develop five fold ministry teams in your church	$7.50 donation	
	**MORE BOOKS**		
	God's Vision: A Supernatural Church - Virkler	$8.95	
	49 Lies I Rejected When I Renounced Phariseeism - Virkler	$9.95	
	Release From Religion	$8.95	
	Release From Religion Teacher's Guide	$8.95	

#	TITLE	UNIT PRICE	EXTENDED COST
	Correspondent Student Information	$3.00	
	Church-centered Bible School Training Three catalogs on how to establish an affiliate church-centered Bible school utilizing this curriculum, and offering a B.A. or Master's degree.	$7.50 donation	
	Lamad Curriculum Catalog Listing over 72 courses designed for individual & small group use. These courses lead the learner into guided self-discovery, and interaction with the Holy Spirit.	Free	
	Quarterly Communion With God Newsletter	Donation	
	TOTAL BOOKS	Subtotal	
	Shipping & handling ($4.00 minimum)		
	COD Orders add additional $4.00		
	New York State orders add NYS Sales Tax		
	TOTAL COST		

SHIPPING & HANDLING

Minimum charge $4.00 per order or respective % of subtotal.

  10%   U.S.A.
  14%   Canada
  20%   Rest of World

COD Orders add additional $4.00. Please allow 6-8 weeks for delivery to overseas countries.

MAIL TO:
Communion With God Ministries
1431 Bullis Road
Elma, New York 14059

MONEY BACK GUARANTEE:
If you are not completely satisfied with these materials, you may return them within 30 days in resalable condition and receive a full refund on the cost of the book.

Prices are Subject to Change Without Notice.

METHOD OF PAYMENT

☐ Check   ☐ Visa   ☐ Master Card   ☐ COD

Card Number	Exp. Date

Card Holder's name (please print)

Signature

Make checks payable to Communion With God Ministries **in American currency drawn on a U.S. bank or use a Postal Money Order in U.S. funds.**